HOW TO SURVIVE
YOUR FIRST TRIP IN THE WILD

HOW TO SURVIVE YOUR FIRST TRIP IN THE WILD

BACKPACKING FOR BEGINNERS

Paul Magnanti

ROCKRIDGE PRESS

Interior and Cover Designer: Darren Samuel
Photo Art Director / Art Manager: Sue Bischofberger
Editor: Justin Hartung
Production Editor: Ashley Polikoff
Illustrations: Remie Geoffroi
Author photo courtesy of © Josh Zapin

ISBN: Print 978-1-64152-682-1 | eBook 978-1-64152-683-8

With much love to Joan,
who always supported and believed in me.

CONTENTS

INTRODUCTION

One sunny weekend in New Hampshire, a friend took me on
my first backpacking trip. I had done day hikes and camping
trips while in the Boy Scouts, but I'd never been backpacking.
I was 25 pounds overweight, and my gear included a knife
more appropriate for Bear Grylls, a flashlight with a big 6-volt
battery, and enough canned goods to stock a 7-Eleven. We
planned to hike only 12 miles, so how difficult could that be?

The first day, I was out of breath as we hiked but enjoyed
the sunshine and the fantastic views—until we realized we'd
forgotten the map. My friend told me he remembered the
way and that I shouldn't worry. Around 6:00 p.m., though,
we arrived at the same campsite we had used the previous
night. We'd hiked in a 12-mile circle! We set up the tent, didn't
bother eating dinner, and collapsed into our sleeping bags.

On this first, mistake-prone trip, I got lost and carried way
too much, but by the end, I enjoyed myself thoroughly. I was
lucky. A few more disasters such as bad weather, getting
even more lost, carrying additional weight, or injuring myself
because I wasn't physically prepared could have easily shifted
the experience from a formative moment in my life to something I'd never do again.

Instead, this weekend in New Hampshire was the beginning of my love of backpacking. Skip ahead two years to a

sunny day in August. I'm on the summit of Mount Katahdin in Maine with a big smile on my face because I had just completed a five-month journey by thru-hiking the more than two-thousand-mile-long Appalachian Trail.

My goal in writing this book is to inspire the same passion for the wild in you that I developed after my first backpacking trip. The tools and suggestions I will go over in the coming pages will help you avoid the same mistakes that I made. By being better prepared, you'll be able to relax and enjoy a few chuckles along the way. Ultimately, the goal is to get you on the trail, where much of the real learning happens.

If this book is your first step in exploring the wild, I hope it will encourage you to explore deserts, mountains, woods, and other areas that make being out in nature a rewarding experience.

And trust me: You'll survive.

Happy trails!

How to Use This Book

This book is designed to walk you through the steps needed to plan your first short backpacking trip from start to finish in the beautiful, varied wilderness of the United States. You will learn how to pick the best destination, maneuver the difficult permit process, and navigate trails. The basics, including how to set up and break camp; how to stay warm, dry, and well-fed for a weekend of hiking; and the seven Leave No Trace principles are also covered in depth.

Along the way, you'll find quick "how to survive" tips for everything from getting lost to the best way to store your equipment. The end of the book is packed with camping checklists, ideas for your first trip, and more.

Loaded with everything you need to know to hit the trail, this book will put you at ease about the idea of going off into the wild for two or three nights. The unknown can be intimidating; there are no tigers, but there may be (mountain) lions and bears. As it turns out, those bears aren't too big of a concern after all.

"**I just walked. I was *very* happy.**"

—Bill Bryson, *A Walk in the Woods*

1

PLANNING YOUR TRIP

All backpacking journeys start with a single step—but it's not the one you think. Whether it's a multi-week journey on the Appalachian Trail or a quick weekend getaway out of the city, your first step will be planning your trip. Before you set out on the trail, you'll need to pick a destination, figure out your itinerary, gather the appropriate equipment, plan a route, procure the proper permits, book campsites, and figure out how to get to the trailhead.

If the idea of preparing for a satisfying, safe trip feels daunting, fear not. This chapter will break down your first steps into easy-to-tackle tasks. Before you know it, you'll get to the fun stuff—enjoying the great outdoors on your first backpacking adventure.

Creating a Plan

While you might have romantic notions of packing some bread and tea and hopping a fence à la famed naturalist John Muir, a thoughtful itinerary is key to a safe, rewarding experience. Take the time to plan. Incidents that result from poorly planned trips may make for funny stories later on, but they can be unpleasant or even downright dangerous in the moment.

How far in advance do you need to plan your trip? If your first backpacking adventure is something ambitious and complicated for beginners, such as Grand Canyon National Park, you'll need to book permits months in advance. But if you're heading to a local wilderness area or state park, you could get the self-signed permit at the trailhead the very morning you start the trip. In addition to getting permits, you might need to secure time off with your employer. And, of course, going with a group will require even more coordination.

For your first trip, keep it simple. Consider the length and skill level of the hike, the travel time required, seasonal concerns, the cost, and the ease of securing permits. If your first trip requires more than a month of logistic preparation, it's probably more complicated than it should be. Our previous example of the Grand Canyon would be a bucket list trip for an experienced backpacker; a local outdoor area will be less stressful and easier to plan overall.

Ideally, your first backpacking destination shouldn't be more than a few hours' drive away, with easily procured permits and a trip length of two or three days. This will make it easier to plan and coordinate. And, if Murphy's Law (meaning, anything that can go wrong will go wrong) rears its ugly head, you can simply go home, reassess, and try again another time.

When planning your first trip, physical preparation is just as important as figuring out logistics. Being active not only helps you achieve good physical conditioning for your upcoming backpacking weekend but also helps with overall physical and mental health. Daily hikes are ideal but not realistic for everyone. Making running, biking, gym workouts, or active sports such as basketball a regular part of your routine will help you maintain physical fitness. Chapter 3 (page 47) covers this important topic more extensively.

Other factors to consider include the destination, trip goals, length of trip, budget, steps needed to procure permits, planning where to camp, group dynamics, and the season.

Choosing a Destination

Do you want to see the famed Red Rock Desert of Utah? Perhaps you're hoping to enjoy the brilliance of New England's fall colors. Or maybe you're aiming to crest a high mountain pass deep in the Colorado Rockies. Destinations fuel backpacking dreams. But unless you're lucky enough to live near one of these dream destinations, you may need to temper your expectations for your first trip. You can always work your way up to your bucket-list adventures.

So, where to go first? You'll find a list of **great beginner hikes by state** plus advice on seasonal planning in the back of this book (page 115). Remember, when choosing your first destination, consider these factors:

Your first trip should be close-by and require permits that are easy to get. As discussed in the planning section (page 7), keeping your first trip simple means having fewer things to arrange. Extra steps—such as coordinating intricate permits and long-distance travel—could make your first trip more complicated than it needs to be. Nearby trips are oftentimes less expensive, too.

A beginner's trail should have moderate mileage and elevation gain. An ideal first trip length is 2 to 3 days or 20 to 30 total miles. Also, make sure your first trip is not on trails that are too steep, or you will feel every pound in your pack during the climb. An excellent baseline for moderate elevation gain is no more than 2,000 feet per 5 to 10 miles of hiking. Looking for something easier? Try trails with a 700- to 800-foot gain per 5 to 10 miles. Again, refer to the list at the back of this book for some ideas (page 115).

Consider the abilities and experience of the group. Solo wilderness travel can be rewarding for the experienced backpacker. But for your first few trips, it's best to go with a friend or two. You can also split up shared gear such as a stove, tent, or water filter to avoid doubling up on equipment. Tailor the trip to the least experienced or physically able person of the group.

Too long or too steep of a trip for a less prepared group member means a less enjoyable trip for everyone. If possible, consider inviting a more experienced backpacker on the trip. Many experienced backcountry travelers enjoy spending time and sharing the experience with new backpackers. On the other hand, try not to travel with a group that's too large. More than four people tends to overcomplicate a trip. Breaks become longer, logistics more difficult (two cars versus one, for example), and your permit might limit the number of people per campsite.

Factor in the time of the year. Late spring through early fall are ideal times for beginners (with some exceptions, such as desert areas). Outside of these prime seasons, you'll need gear and skills beyond the comfort level of most beginners.

Consider the terrain. Hiking in the desert or high alpine areas provides some memorable scenery, but it also comes with specific challenges such as sun exposure and the need to carry more water. For your first trip, consider an area more benign like a mainly wooded environment with ample water.

Budgeting for Your Trip

How much will your first trip cost? As usual, the answer depends on a variety of factors.

If you are taking a trip to a distant national park, then the cost of airfare, a car rental, permit fees, and possibly lodging will make the trip expensive. But if you'll be backpacking in a nearby state forest for a weekend, your only expenses will be gas and food. If you need to get a permit, make sure you include any state park entry and campsite fees in your budget.

SPRING SNOW

In the Pacific Northwest, the Rockies, and many parts of the Northeast, snow lingers well into spring.

Colloquially known as "rotten snow," this type of snow is often mushy, difficult to walk on, and makes for slower travel. Even if there isn't snow, the trail conditions will likely be muddy. Expect slower travel at higher elevations. In the Rockies and other mountainous areas, spring is avalanche season. Wise backcountry travelers adjust their plans to avoid these types of conditions. Plan a lower elevation trip in the foothills, or delay your trip until the summer.

Finally, you might not have a choice. Many trail organizations request that backcountry users avoid the local "mud season." The terrain is more susceptible to environmental damage from foot traffic when the conditions are sloppy. Please respect this request and help preserve our public lands.

Gear will also affect your initial trip expenses. Those on a budget might be able to be able to rely on things already in their closet, while others may want to stock up on potentially pricey lightweight gear. Assuming you're starting from scratch and want good, sturdy gear, you can easily outfit yourself for under $2,000. For bargain hunters, this budget can easily be cut in half. Chapter 2 (page 15) will cover gear and clothing options, types, and concerns in more detail.

Planning Campsites

You've planned your destination, gathered the gear, and marked the dates on your calendar. Now it's time to pick your campsite. Most backcountry offices require you to know where you want to camp before they issue a permit. If your preferred campsite is not available, the backcountry office will work with you to find a suitable site that still works with your itinerary.

If you're traveling to a national park or higher-use wilderness area, your campsite choices will be limited to designated sites or zones. National and state parks are typically more regulated than United States Forest Service (USFS) or Bureau of Land Management (BLM) areas, and they have more campsite amenities such as outhouses, firepits, or designated areas to set up your tent.

In more obscure or lightly managed areas, you can "disperse camp," meaning you may camp anywhere along the terrain, assuming you are following the seven Leave No Trace principles. Camping in designated campsites makes picking a site easier, while dispersed camping offers more choice. For your first trips, using designated campsites is simpler and requires less planning.

So, how do you find campsites? Online or print guides often list campsites to choose from, including information about key features like local lakes or even sunset views. On most maps, a tent symbol indicates a campsite location. Later in this book (page 81), you'll learn how to find the best areas for dispersed camping on maps. Finally, land agency offices are usually happy to give suggestions for campsites in the areas they serve. If you have any questions about a specific site, regulation, or trail conditions, give them a call.

When picking a campsite, factor in the amount of daylight available, your pace, and the amount of mileage your group can cover in a day. Try to be at your campsite at least an hour before sunset; you can easily find the sunset time for an area with a simple online search.

As mentioned earlier in the book (page 4), most beginners find between 8 and 10 miles per day with moderate elevation gain to be a good pace that balances a sense of accomplishment with a realistic goal. How fast will you hike these miles? Most people hike at 2 miles per hour with an additional 30 minutes for every 1,000 feet of elevation gain.

Terrain Considerations

Many beginner backpackers choose campsites in wide-open meadows. But meadows are usually located in valleys, where cold air settles; they can also be wetter, meaning you may have to deal with insects. Instead, look for sites surrounded by

HOW TO SURVIVE
WHEN YOUR GROUP CAN'T AGREE

In an ideal world, every evening on the trail would finish with a "Kumbaya" sing-along around a campfire with our fellow wilderness travelers. But the world is more complicated, and people disagree.

Planning trips for a group increases the potential for conflict. Collaborate, and don't dictate. What type of trip best fits your group? Something challenging or more easygoing? Desert, mountains, or deep forest? Working together as a group to agree on an initial plan makes conflict less likely during the trip.

Even the most collaborative groups may disagree about scheduling, trip goals, physical abilities, and destination choices. Balance and compromise make for a more enjoyable trip for all. If your trip partner needs to get back earlier on a Sunday, plan a lower mileage day so you can enjoy the trip and not worry about the time of return. And then suggest the next trip will be more ambitious.

Or, if the difference in physical ability is causing pre-trip conflict, plan a more leisurely trip for the first outing, but gently suggest more physical preparation for the second outing.

trees; they're often protected from the wind, a little warmer, and have ground cover that provides more comfortable sleeping and helps insulate your sleeping pad.

Another common rookie mistake is camping near a lake, which is tempting from an aesthetic standpoint. But lakeside camping offers similar issues to camping in a meadow. Also, since so many people love to camp near lakes, these sites fall prey to creatures that will try to steal your food.

Ideally, try not to camp at the absolute highest or lowest point in the general area. Campsites at higher elevations tend to be windy. Too low? Again, cold air settles. Also, it's important to avoid camping at the bottom of a runoff (as rain travels downhill) or near dead trees (widely known as "widowmakers"). Finally, do not camp where there are lots of roots, rocks, and other debris, which can lead to rips or gradual wear and tear on your tent.

Getting Your Permits

Consider obtaining a permit the first navigation challenge for any backpacking trip—one you'll definitely survive. Depending on which land agency you're dealing with, permits can vary significantly in cost and procedure.

Begin by visiting the land agency website, and check out the web-based resources and apps listed at the back of this book (page 130). National parks, the United States Forest Service, the Bureau of Land Management, state parks, and other land agencies typically list the procedure for obtaining a permit online.

Unfortunately, there is no uniform procedure for securing a permit. Even among national park units, the methods differ. Some parks allow online booking, while others require you to call in, mail a permit fee, or even fax a permit request.

Most national parks require an entrance fee, plus an additional camping permit fee per party for the week. The United States Forest Service wilderness areas or the Bureau of Land Management usually charge minimal fees (sometimes they're free) for a backcountry permit, which is obtained at the trailhead. Be sure to bring cash. Fees in state parks vary by state and are often higher than federal fees.

HOW TO SURVIVE
DEALING WITH MURPHY'S LAW

No matter how well you plan, Murphy's Law will kick in at some point. Maybe you forgot the permit at home. Or a bear encounter closed down a trail you planned to take to a campsite. Or a fire ban means you can't cook your famous trail stew over the campfire coals just like your grandfather did.

While planning won't eliminate these potential issues, it will provide the flexibility to deal with unexpected problems. Take the campsite snafu. If you've pre-planned your campsites, you're probably familiar with the map and know how to contact the backcountry office. No problem—you'll get a different campsite. In the case of the fire ban, a well-prepared backpacker knows how to use a modern camp stove to make a delicious dinner.

Proper planning, a flexible mind-set, and a sense of humor all help in dealing with Mr. Murphy. And when he does inevitably raise his head, don't fret. Just embrace it as part of the adventure.

THE SEVEN
LEAVE NO TRACE PRINCIPLES

Finally, before you do any further planning for your trip, familiarize yourself with the seven Leave No Trace principles (LNT). These principles are as important to the twenty-first-century backcountry experience as a good map and proper shoes. Keep these principles in mind on any trip to our natural lands. Following these practices helps preserve and protect our wild spaces. It also makes for an enjoyable experience for you, other visitors, and the wildlife that call these lands home.

The seven LNT principles are:

- **Plan ahead and prepare.**

- **Travel and camp on durable surfaces.**

- **Dispose of waste properly.**

- **Leave what you find.**

- **Minimize campfire impacts (be careful with fire).**

- **Respect wildlife.**

- **Be considerate of other visitors.**

In the chapters ahead, we'll explore these concepts in more detail. For more information on the LNT principles and the Leave No Trace organization, visit www.lnt.org.

"Carry as little as possible,
but choose that little with care."

—Earl Shaffer, the first Appalachian Trail thru-hiker

2

GEARING UP

Gear is the topic many new and experienced backpackers tend to worry about the most. After all, gear can be expensive, and the choices can easily overwhelm a person. Will the gear you purchase perform as needed out on the trail? Will you be able to afford all the equipment you need? How do you prepare for unpredictable weather?

Don't worry. Backpacking is a pastime that lends itself to simplicity, making it an ideal passion for those seeking a less frantic, less complicated vacation. Do your research and you'll find that the gear you need can be affordable, simple, and compact.

Before purchasing any gear for your first trip, review the First Trip Checklist at the back of this book (page 125). In fact, just take the list with you.

The basic "tools of the trade," like the appropriate pack, stove, or footwear, make it easier for any outdoor enthusiast to safely and comfortably experience wild places. It's important to find gear that will last because once you experience these places for the first time, you'll want to return.

Carefully considered gear, along with knowledge, planning, and research, work together to make a backcountry trip run smoothly. But gear is just one part of the trip. We use gear to enjoy the outdoors; we don't go outdoors to enjoy gear.

Clothing

The ideal backpacking clothes should feel as comfortable and practical as your favorite pair of jeans. If you day hike or camp, you probably already have the clothing you need for backpacking. If you're new to backpacking, here is overview of what you'll need.

The quick and dirty clothing rule is: no cotton. Cotton may be comfortable, but it loses any ability to insulate when it gets wet and can even pull heat from your body, which can cause hypothermia. Sweaty cotton undergarments or socks can cause chafing, blisters, and all-around discomfort. Leave the blue jeans and a cotton T-shirt in the car for after the trip.

For most hiking, you'll want to wear synthetic shorts or long pants, plus a synthetic short- or long-sleeved shirt. (Note that long pants and sleeves help protect you from the sun and prevent bug bites from mosquitos or ticks and rashes caused by poison oak or poison ivy.)

You don't have to spend a lot of money to get this clothing; in fact, you might already have a pair of nylon running shorts or swim trunks that would work well. Synthetic T-shirts are reasonably inexpensive. Polyester shirts can be found easily at thrift stores; they may not be the height of fashion, but they're cheap and effective. On your feet, wear wool or synthetic socks. Cotton socks retain moisture and can cause blisters—not anyone's idea of backcountry fun.

The one exception to the no cotton rule is a bandana. Just get one. Simply put, the humble bandana has almost limitless uses. It can provide sun protection on your neck, or can be used to soak up sweat; on a hot day, dipping a bandana in cool water and wearing it on your head is heavenly. It can also be used as a first-aid tool; the bandana makes a handy sling, bandage, tourniquet, or emergency signal. It's also useful for cleaning cooking pots, wiping down tents, storing leftover food, straining silty water, or swatting bugs.

The Layer Principle

During inclement weather, be prepared to dress in layers. Though there are differing opinions on the number of layers that you should wear, four layers generally serve beginning backpackers well on outings from late spring to early fall.

The four basics of the layer principle include:

An inner base layer to keep your core warm. These are your shorts, shirt, undergarments, and socks. During cool weather, wear a thermal top and bottom layers ("long johns") and possibly a hat for sun protection.

A middle layer to retain body heat when active. Opt for a light fleece or a wind shirt (a lighter, more breathable version of the classic windbreaker). Colder weather typically warrants gloves or mittens and a warm beanie-style hat. The gloves or mittens need not be fancy; a simple pair of gloves found at a hardware store's checkout counter should suffice. Gloves provide more dexterity; mittens are warmer.

An outer shell layer to keep out the rain and other precipitation. Modern rain jackets and pants are lighter and less

LAYERING FOR THE DESERT

Layering for the desert means more than just wearing shorts, a T-shirt, and a running cap. Deserts are often at higher elevations, some almost a mile high. They also cool down at night, and rain or snow is a possibility.

Your layering strategy is similar to the classic four-layer strategy we just covered. But those same layers are used differently in desert climates. Rain gear doubles as wind protection. And though a heavy down coat might be overkill for Utah in July, you'll be happy you packed a light fleece once that sun goes down.

Water is critical in the desert. Drink water often, eat salty snacks such as chips, and seek shade for the hottest part of the day. If you are not an experienced desert traveler, avoid desert hikes in the summer.

bulky than the rubber suits found in most discount stores. You can use anything from an expensive Gore-Tex jacket to a simple coated nylon pullover. Though ponchos provide ideal ventilation versus other rain garment options, they work best in a sheltered environment with less wind. In addition to a rain jacket, rain mittens or gloves will protect your hands during inclement weather and provide some additional warmth. For those on a budget, heavier, rubber dishwashing gloves are a less expensive alternative.

A down or synthetic layer for cooler nights in camp or colder rest stops. Colloquially known as a "puffy," this layer is light, compresses well, and provides the most warmth per ounce of any clothing item. Do not wear this layer when actively hiking because your sweat will compromise its insulation properties. Note that this layer takes longer to dry.

Footwear

Notice that the title of this section is "footwear" and not "boots." Insisting on boots for backpacking is an outmoded idea. The lighter weight of modern backpacks, improved trail maintenance, and better trail shoe design mean boots are no longer necessary for most backpackers.

Put simply, the lighter your footwear, the less strain you'll put on your body, and the more comfortable you'll be while walking. And unless you have a specific foot issue or your ankles roll easily, the old chestnut about the improved ankle protection provided by boots has been debunked. In fact, some

SUN PROTECTION

Whether you're hiking in the desert, high alpine areas, or the High Plains, sun protection is critical. Slathering yourself with sunscreen, however, isn't the best approach for an overnight trip. Sunscreen tends to clog pores, pick up dirt, and requires regular reapplication. Wearing appropriate clothing is more effective, less hassle, and easier than using sunscreen. It's also the method many medical organizations prefer.

Some strategies for using clothing for sun protection include:

- A **wide-brimmed hat** to shade your face and the back of your neck.

- **Sunglasses** to protect your eyes from strain, sun-blindness, and UV damage. Most sunglasses have UVA and UVB protection. Safety glasses are light, durable, inexpensive, and are ANSI-certified to established standards.

- **A long-sleeved button-down** shirt protects your neck and arms and provides ventilation in hot weather, too.

- If you have particularly fair skin, **long pants** will protect your legs from the sun. Long pants are also ideal for brushy terrain.

- Some backpackers **hike with an umbrella.** Though the technique can work well, it's best to try this out once you dial in your gear.

If you decide to use sunscreen, a travel-size bottle is enough for a typical weekend. Apply on the ears, face, arms, neck, and legs about one hour before you start hiking for the day. You'll also want to reapply every few hours. Remember that thorough application is key to a sunscreen's effectiveness.

studies even show that boots may hinder the strengthening of ankles.

Because shoes fit each person differently, shop at a brick-and-mortar outdoor store rather than online. A well-stocked store will have plenty of options and experienced staff to help find the best shoe for you.

For most people, trail shoes work well. They are basically a low-cut hiking boot that provide support and tread without the extra weight. Trail shoes won't sap your energy like traditional boots and are usually cheaper.

Note that unless you are blessed with perfect feet, the factory inserts found in most shoes and boots are inadequate. The staff at a good outdoor store should be able to suggest thicker inserts that are appropriate for your foot and gait.

Be sure to break in new shoes by using them often, beginning at least a month before your trip. Wear a loaded day pack or book bag and take hikes in the woods or through the neighborhood. If you don't live in an area with steep climbs, add stair climbing into your routine. Get a sense of how the shoes feel while you're walking. Are you experiencing any obvious pain or discomfort? Better to find out now rather than on your trip. Most outdoor stores have a return policy that allows you to return the shoes within a certain time frame.

Backpacks

A backpack carries your shelter, bed, kitchen, and pantry. Think of it as your portable home while out in the backcountry.

The ideal backpack will carry your gear comfortably and, of course, fit you correctly.

There are three basic pack types to choose from:

External frame packs feature a ladder-like frame to which the main pack body is attached. Your tent, sleeping bag, and pad will also attach to the frame. External frame packs distribute weight evenly—meaning they're ideal for carrying heavy loads on maintained trail—and are relatively inexpensive. They tend to be heavier than other packs and have limited adjustment options, which can lead to discomfort on hikes. Additionally, items lashed to the side can easily snag

on brush or trees and become damaged. It's a good choice for those on a budget, but most people switch over to internal frame packs after a few hikes.

Internal frame packs look a bit like duffel bags, and you'll find them displayed prominently in most outdoor stores. An aluminum or carbon frame provides structure within the pack. These bags also carry weight well and have a slim profile for more comfortable walking.

Frameless rucksacks look similar to internal frame packs, but are not suggested for most beginners, as there's no direct support built into the pack (the gear within provides structure). To use this type of pack effectively, a person needs to have a very light gear system dialed in correctly and be comfortable with a more minimalist kit.

Pack fit depends on the individual and can vary based on body type, musculature, and gender. As with shoes, purchase your pack at a well-stocked outdoor store that has an experienced staff to help you.

A piece of conventional wisdom that has held up over the years: Make your pack the last thing you purchase. Only after you assemble all your other equipment will you know which pack will hold your gear, carry it comfortably, and fit you well.

As for size, if you buy an internal frame pack, look for one that carries roughly 60 liters. It's not too heavy, but it's large enough for most backpackers' needs, with room for a small bear canister. Also, you can find them at most price points.

Once you've packed your gear (I'll discuss how to do so in the next chapter, page 57), take it out for a trial run with your shoes to make sure there are no issues before you hit the trail. If the pack isn't comfortable, make adjustments or go back to the outdoor store and exchange it for a different pack. A good-fitting pack is key to an enjoyable backpacking trip.

Tents and Shelters

A well-situated shelter will shield you from rain, snow, and sleet. It will also protect you from insects and provide privacy in a group setting.

Some minimalist and solo backpackers prefer to camp without a tent, using a simple tarp only in rain. Others prefer a palatial "Taj Mahal" that's comfortable in all conditions but heavy to carry.

Here are the three most common types of shelter:

Tarp or tarp-like shelters can be square, rectangular, or shaped like a pyramid. Fans of these shelters tend to be minimalist backpackers who pack light and do longer mileage days. Tarps require more skill to use than tents, but their light weight and simplicity make them attractive to more experienced outdoor enthusiasts.

Single-wall shelters are constructed with a single wall of fabric. Lighter than a double-wall tent, these tents are more susceptible to condensation. They're best for generally dry conditions (e.g., the Rockies or the deserts of the Southwest). Many specialty lightweight manufacturers design single-wall tents, and they tend be more expensive than double-wall tents.

Double-wall shelters consist of a predominantly mesh body plus a separate waterproof rainfly that's attached during inclement weather. Double-wall shelters usually have better ventilation than single-wall shelters and are less expensive. They tend to be heavier and bulkier as well.

Most shelters are available in two configurations: freestanding or non-freestanding. Freestanding shelters rely on poles rather than stakes for their structure (although stakes are needed to keep them from blowing away). Non-freestanding shelters need both the tent poles and stakes to provide structural integrity. Typically, freestanding shelters can be set up more quickly, but they're heavier and more expensive.

A rule of thumb: If a manufacturer claims it's a "three-person" tent, that typically means it's realistically comfortable for two adults. And a one-person tent? Just barely enough room for you and your sleeping bag.

If this is your first backpacking trip, I suggest you use a tent instead of a tarp. Tents are easier to set up and can fit two people. Be sure to bring a three-season tent if you can. A four-season tent (a tent with steep walls primarily designed to shed snow in winter) is overkill for most trips, plus it's heavier and has less ventilation. A double-wall tent makes an economical and versatile first purchase. There are many well-built and affordable three-person, five-pound tents that two people can easily share.

Some people will also bring a plastic ground cloth for their tents. If you are rough on your gear, using a tarp, or are camping in rough terrain, a ground cloth can be useful. But you probably won't need one; modern tents have well-built floors, and most feature a bathtub design that helps prevent water from getting inside.

Sleeping Bags and Pads

Your sleeping bag keeps you warm at night and is often the last line of defense when you are cold and wet. So, more than any other piece of gear, it makes sense to purchase the highest-quality sleeping bag that you can afford. If used frequently, a high-quality bag will last a decade or more, and most bag technology rarely becomes outdated. Purchase a high-quality bag initially, and you likely won't need to purchase another one, even as you upgrade or swap out other gear over the years.

Backpacker sleeping bags are mummy-shaped to maximize weight and thermal efficiency. Most backpackers find a 20 degrees Fahrenheit bag (suitable down to 20 degrees Fahrenheit or −7 degrees Celsius) to be the most versatile for 3-season use. Even in warmer climates, the nights can be cool.

Sleeping bags contain two types of fill material: synthetic and down (goose). Synthetics are heavier and bulkier, but they're less expensive than down bags. Synthetic bags resist moisture better when conditions are wet as well. Down bags are more expensive but are less bulky, lighter, more durable, and tend to be a bit warmer. The one catch: When a down bag is wet, it's almost useless; the down collapses and doesn't provide insulation. This factor is more of a drawback in, say, the Pacific Northwest than in the dry climate of Colorado. Despite this, many experienced backpackers prefer down bags overall. If you do get one, carry it in a stuff sack lined with a garbage bag.

An increasingly popular alternative to sleeping bags, a sleeping quilt is superficially similar to a sleeping bag but doesn't have a hood or a bottom. The backpacker drapes a quilt over their body to retain warmth. The main advantage of a quilt is that it is lightweight. As with a tarp, quilts are mainly used by experienced backpackers.

Under your sleeping bag, a sleeping pad will keep you comfortable and provide further insulation from the cold ground. The thicker pads have a better R-value (resistance value), which means more insulation. But these pads also can be bulker, heavier, and sometimes pricier. The two basic types of sleeping pads are closed cell foam (CCF) pads and inflatable mattresses.

CCF pads are light and inexpensive, but they're also bulky, and many find them to be less comfortable than inflatable pads. The pads range from the classic "blue foamer" found in many discount stores to newer style foam pads that, though more expensive, have a good R-value and are more comfortable.

A good choice that balances weight, bulk, comfort, R-value, and price is the classic Therm-A-Rest inflatable pads by Cascade Designs. These pads are comfortable, somewhat expensive, and on the heavier side compared with CCF pads. There are newer insulated air pads that are very light but more expensive and less durable. When properly maintained, they'll last for many years. Store brand versions of this popular model have similar attributes but typically cost less than the brand name version, too.

Food and Cookware

A typical backpacker burns more than 4,000 calories a day on the trail. Food is fuel, and the proper amount of fuel plus the tools to prepare it are critical when out in the wild.

Camp food used to consist of Spam, canned beef stew, canned beans, and pancake mix, all cooked over a campfire. Luckily, there are now easier-to-cook, lighter-to-carry foods for backpacking trips that still provide the calories you need. Modern backpacking stoves also cook food more quickly, efficiently, and in a more environmentally friendly way than a campfire.

Keep It Light

On a short first trip, packing lightweight food that's high in calories is not as critical, but it's still good to keep these concepts in mind. A can of tuna won't hurt, but carrying five cans of "big and meaty" chili might.

To keep your pack light, it's worth considering the freeze-dried meals found at most outdoor stores; they're light and require only some boiling water to cook. Sure, they're expensive—and the serving sizes claimed on packaging can be unrealistic—but the convenience and ease of use make them an excellent choice. And for a quick weekend trip, the cost may not be as important.

But if you are on a budget, your local grocery store has many items that work great for backpacking meals. Instant oatmeal, mac and cheese, candy bars, nuts, and raisins are foods that are lightweight and pack a caloric punch without breaking the bank.

Another alternative is to make your own dehydrated meals. With a food dehydrator, you can make fruit leathers and dehydrated soups, chili, sauces, and more. Obviously, this brings its own budget, time, and space challenges.

People often tout MREs (meals ready to eat, aka military rations) as a good option. But they have excessive packaging, are a bit heavy, and can be somewhat expensive if you don't buy in bulk. Still, if you break down the packaging and throw the food in a resealable food storage bag, MREs can be a convenient and quick meal for an overnighter.

How Much Food to Pack

Whatever strategy you decide to go with for food, the rule of thumb is to pack 2 pounds of food per person for each day, and be sure that the food you've packed contains about 100 calories per ounce. You will burn the calories while hiking, so plan accordingly. Backpacking is a great time to indulge in your favorite foods.

One more quick note: Rather than stopping for a long lunch, it's better to "graze" all day. This is especially true on long hikes. Munch on your trail mix, eat some cheese, and nosh on that bagel with peanut butter. While backpacking, you will be burning a lot of fuel. Stoke that furnace.

Sample Menu

Here is a sample menu for a three-day, two-night trip using food bought at a grocery store and an outdoor store. The menu might sound simple at first, but when you are hiking miles throughout the day you'll want basic food. Keep it simple. Bring lightweight food that takes less time to prepare in camp, takes up less room in your pack, and keeps the logistics of cooking easy for your first trip. As more than one outdoor sage has stated, "Hunger makes the best sauce." Perhaps hold off on channeling your inner Julia Child to create some more elaborate fare until you are more comfortable in an outdoor setting.

Day One

Breakfast: At home, before hitting the trail. Eat enough food to sustain you for the morning, but not so heavy you will feel bloated on the trail. A two-egg breakfast burrito works well.

Snacks: Bagel with peanut butter, trail mix (raisins, nuts, M&Ms), granola bars, cheese.

Dinner: Mac and cheese with tuna, powdered milk for mac and cheese preparation, hot chocolate.

HOW TO SURVIVE
STORING YOUR GEAR

One of the benefits of backpacking is that the gear takes up very little storage space. Even city dwellers in tiny apartments can find a place for it. If you have a corner in your bedroom or even space under the bed, you can easily store all your gear.

Clean all your equipment thoroughly before putting it into storage. Dry out all the gear and remove any debris. Wet gear stored improperly may develop mold and dirt-filled packs or shelters can wear down quickly. Washing all your hiking clothes will extend its life. If possible, dry clothes on a drying rack instead of in a dryer to preserve the wool and synthetic clothing.

"Puffy" clothing and your sleeping bag should be cleaned sparingly and only when needed. Once per year of active use is a good rule of thumb. Too much washing can damage the insulation in these expensive pieces of gear and clothing. Wash them by hand using specific cleaning products found at outdoor stores. Dry on low heat with tennis balls to prevent clumping.

Once your gear is clean and dry, store it all (including clothing) in your backpack. In addition to taking up less space, you'll be ready to go for future trips.

Important exceptions: Do not store your shoes, puffy layer, or sleeping bag in your pack. Your shoes are typically bulky and dirty. Store them in a closet or similar area by a door. Compression can damage your puffy jacket or sleeping bag in just a few weeks. Hang your jacket in the closet. Store your sleeping bag loose in a large cotton laundry bag. Many sleeping bags come with this type of container. These bags allow the insulation to breathe a bit without compressing it.

Day Two

Breakfast: Two packs instant oatmeal, trail mix, instant coffee packet.

Snacks: Beef jerky, dried fruit, cheese, bagel with peanut butter, trail mix.

Dinner: Freeze-dried beef stew, herbal tea.

Day Three

Breakfast: Eggs with freeze-dried green peppers and cheese, coffee packet.

Snacks: Trail mix and cheese.

Dinner: You completed your first backpacking trip! Time for pizza and a cold beverage to celebrate.

Cookware Basics

In addition to food, you'll need to pack a stove and a simple cookset to prepare your food. Modern backpacking stoves are marvelous little devices that don't weigh much or take up much space.

There are various backpacking stove types, but the most popular is a canister stove. Not to be confused with camp stoves that use green propane bottles, these stoves use small isobutane canisters. The stove and canister typically weigh less than eight ounces, are thermally efficient, and heat food and water quickly. A stove of this type can be found at outdoor stores; budget versions are available from online retailers.

Less common are white gas stoves (Coleman fuel), which are typically used more for mountaineering and winter treks. Alcohol stoves also have a niche among lightweight backpackers but are becoming less common because of open-flame bans in the increasingly dry American West.

What about cooking on a campfire? Aside from the fact that fires are often not allowed in many areas, a campfire can take too long for cooking. They're also not very environmentally sound, especially when backpackers use scarce wood. However, in a permitted safe area with plenty of downed wood, sitting around a small campfire can be enjoyable at the end of the day.

A cookset can be elementary: You only need a pot for boiling water (and to eat out of if going minimalist), a bowl, and a large spoon. A general rule of thumb is to boil one liter of water per person. A one-liter pot is good for one person, and a two-liter pot can boil enough water for two people. Inexpensive pots are readily available.

Cleanup

Cleaning your cookware need not be difficult. Cook your meals on the soupy side for easy cleanup. Clean out any excess food by swishing a bit of water around the pan and wiping it down with your bandana.

Do not use soap. Even the products marked as biodegradable are not in line with Leave No Trace practices. Instead, bring along a few resealable, heavy-duty sandwich or freezer bags to pack out food scraps and other waste. Some of the more hard-core backpackers advocate drinking the cleaning water from your pot to avoid leaving any food particles behind. If the idea of drinking meat-flavored water does not sound appealing, be sure all food particles are removed and pack them out. Then spread (broadcast) the water over a dispersed area at least 200 feet from any water source.

Beverages and Water Containers

There are many choices for backcountry beverages. Water should be your primary beverage. You'll need it to cook your meals, stay hydrated, and maintain your energy level. Drink mixes add flavor to water and make it more palatable. These pack easily and are not expensive.

Carry water in water bottles or water bladders like those by the well-known CamelBak brand.

Repurposed disposable water bottles that are light and easy to pack can be used instead of store-bought backpacking bottles. The advantage of water bottles, besides the price, is that they are easy to refill and allow you to more easily monitor your water intake than a bladder that is inside your pack and out of sight. A useful adjunct to a water bottle is a collapsible water container about a liter in size. Stow this container in your pack when hiking, and use it when you need more capacity in camp or when walking longer stretches without available water supply such as in the desert. A good rule of thumb is to carry one liter of drinking water for every five miles of hiking between water sources. Water sources can include a campsite spigot, a creek, or a lake (you will need to treat water from these sources to ensure that it's safe to drink; I'll discuss this further on the next page). As you gain experience, you can tweak this basic formula for your specific style and pace of hiking.

Many hikers like a water bladder since you can drink water while walking; you "sip and go." The convenience of the water bladder works better for trail running or day hiking. For longer hikes, they tend to be more complicated, heavier, and more prone to fail than water bottles and collapsible containers.

Bringing packets to mix hot drinks such as coffee, tea, cider, or cocoa makes for an excellent way to start a morning or end an evening. On a brisk September morning, a cup of hot coffee seems to make the world just a bit warmer.

Avoid any alcoholic libations on your first few trips. You'll likely be more tired than in your daily life. Alcohol dehydrates you, makes effective judgment more complicated, and could make it difficult to sleep. A nightcap of whiskey works best in cowboy movies and for experienced backpackers who know their physical limitations and comfort zones.

Water Treatment Methods

Unless you're on a very short hike—no more than a mile or two—you will need to find additional water for cooking, drinking, and cleaning. A gallon of water weighs 8 pounds. A typical backpacker can easily use a gallon of water per day. On a 3-day trip, you could potentially need up to 24 pounds in water alone. This is far too much weight to carry unless you are an advanced backpacker on a long desert trip.

Streams, lakes, campsite spigots, or other bodies of water shown on your map are good sources. All water will need to be treated to eradicate contaminants and prevent waterborne illnesses like giardia. If you are downstream of cattle, in a busy area, or if the available water looks scummy, there is a good chance the water will contain illness-causing pathogens.

Water treatment does not have to be complicated, but if you're new to the backcountry you should know the different types of treatment available. Before treating water, always use hand sanitizer.

Mechanical filter. If weight and bulk are not an issue, this tried-and-true water treatment process works well, even if it's a little slower than other methods. It's typically the most expensive method of water treatment.

Squeeze filter. These are lighter, less bulky, and less expensive than mechanical filters, and various models are available from different manufacturers. Instead of the pump used in mechanical filters, these require you to squeeze a small water bladder through the filter. They're an excellent all-around choice for most backcountry use if you're not in an area with silty water (like a desert).

UV pen. This is a battery-powered, pen-shaped device that uses ultraviolet light to treat water. These devices are quicker than other methods of water treatment, but they don't remove particles found in water (use your bandana). They're also somewhat expensive, ineffective with cloudy or silty water, and require batteries.

Chemical treatment. This is a light and inexpensive method compared with filters, but you'll have to wait up to an hour for the water to be treated. It's not as effective in cold weather either. People who choose to treat some, but not all, of their water will typically use a chemical-based treatment. The methods vary between manufacturers. Some treatments involve adding two tablets per liter, a pre-mixed packet of powder, a capful of liquid, or other methods. If you choose to use chemical treatment, read and follow the directions carefully for safe use.

Unless you are backpacking in some remote areas with old mines on Superfund sites (meaning the possibility of chemically toxic groundwater), the water you find in the backcountry will be safe to drink and cook with once treated. These remote areas are not found on beginner routes.

Safety and Hygiene

Safety and hygiene are of the utmost importance when you're backpacking. Here's what you'll need (we'll cover some of these in more detail on page 101).

A map, compass, and possibly a GPS app are necessary for navigating the backcountry. A backpacker should have some level of skill in reading the land and finding destinations. For your initial trip, the ability to identify a trail and major features on a hiking map will be adequate. Many outdoor stores offer basic map reading classes and more advanced classes with field training. And while a GPS-enabled phone and the appropriate navigation app is not critical for navigating, having knowledge of GPS is a skill that is useful at times.

Hiking poles aren't crucial, but they're useful for taking weight off your knees and assisting with steep climbs and rough terrain. Many lightweight shelters are also set up with hiking poles.

An adequate water supply is necessary to maintain health and energy in the backcountry. Don't forget to bring your preferred type of water treatment to prevent waterborne illnesses such as giardia that can cause diarrhea, bloating, and other forms of gastrolienal intestinal distress.

A small (under three ounces) headlamp is superior to a lantern or flashlight. These durable items provide excellent illumination, are handsfree for easy use, and can be found in outdoors stores, discount stores, and even hardware stores. They're especially important for any emergency situations where you need to hike at night.

A basic first-aid kit is an absolute requirement for coping with accidents big and small. Think of it as a seat belt: You don't need it most of the time, but it's essential at critical moments. Depending on how remote the terrain is, you may also want to consider an emergency communication device. The First Aid section of the appendix (page 113) will go into more detail about first aid, emergency equipment, and how to obtain the skills to use this equipment correctly.

Necessary toiletries include a potty trowel (available at outdoor stores), hand sanitizer, and toilet paper. Knowing their proper use is critical for sanitation and helps minimize their impact on the environment. Chapter 6 (page 87) will go into more detail on this process, which is a cause of anxiety for many first-time backpackers.

Fun Stuff

Backpacking gear is not all about practical tools. Though you might find you are too tired on most backpacking days to do more than make camp, cook dinner, and sleep, long summer days in particular provide ample opportunity for activities beyond hiking, eating, sleeping, and repeating.

Some favorite backpacking activities include:

Reading. Pack a favorite book (or bring one on your phone) to read in the quiet of the backcountry. You have the "gift of time"—make use of it.

Journaling. Put yourself in the excellent company of Edward Abbey, Henry David Thoreau, Matsuo Bashō, and Terry Tempest Williams. Something about the outdoors brings out the poet in everyone.

Tenkara fly-fishing. These light, simple-to-use fishing poles from Japan are perfect for backcountry trips.

GEARING UP ON A BUDGET

Backpacking gear and clothing can be expensive. Use these techniques to outfit yourself without spending too much money.

- Use clothing and gear you already have at home. Nylon gym shorts, non-cotton running socks, and possibly your gym shoes will work for well-maintained trails and sometimes beyond. Regular sunglasses are fine.

- Check thrift stores for fleeces, puffy jackets, hiking shirts, etc.

- Purchase cheaper versions of gear at large online retailers. A budget canister stove might be slightly heavier but functions the same and makes a good alternative for money-conscious hikers.

- Buy used, online, or locally. eBay and other gear-specific resources (see page 131) sell used clothing and gear at affordable prices. Local outdoor consignment stores can be competitive, too.

- Purchase gear at the end of the season, when on sale. Buy a down jacket at the start of the spring, for example.

- Check hardware stores for inexpensive clothing that's made for construction or other outdoor activities. The hats, gloves, headlamps, and safety sunglasses work great for backpacking.

- Military surplus stores sell clothing brands such as PolarTec for less than outdoor stores. The clothing might be decked out in military-approved colors, but it is otherwise identical to the fleece and thermal layers sold at mainstream retailers.

- Buy last year's model or factory seconds online or at traditional retailers.

- Use what you already have rather than buying new gear. After a couple of trips, you can determine what works and what you need to replace.

Star-gazing. Take advantage of the lack of light pollution and enjoy the celestial views. Find the International Space Station, identify the planets and constellations, and keep an eye out for comets streaking across the night sky.

Card games. A rainy day? Brew up some tea and play some hearts, poker, or Go Fish to pass the hours away.

Photography and wildlife viewing. This a no-brainer if you're staying at remote campsites in pristine areas with memorable sunsets.

Using Electronics in the Backcountry

Although part of the appeal of backpacking is getting away from technology, phones can be useful for things like GPS navigation apps, taking photos, reading books, or star charts—all of which would have required separate gear a decade ago.

With adjustments to your daily settings, two or three days of casual use such as checking maps, taking photos, reading, and looking up information in an electronic guide will not use up the battery of a phone.

Standard suggestions include putting the phone in airplane mode, setting it to the medium power-saving setting, dimming the screen to the lowest tolerable setting, and avoiding heavy use of the phone. Most users can get about five days of use, although older phone batteries will not last as long.

If you have an older phone or find you are a more frequent electronic user (listening to music or audiobooks or making movies perhaps), a 5,000mAh battery pack only weighs about 4 ounces and will provide 1 or 2 charges.

Do not rely on electronic devices that are susceptible to dirt and moisture. Store the electronics in your pack when the weather seems particularly wet. An effective and inexpensive way to protect your phone is to place it in a resealable zip-top food storage bag. When stored in your pack, the storage bag provides enough protection from all but the heaviest deluge.

If you do use your phone to make calls, try to be discreet and do it away from your fellow trekkers.

"Walking is the best possible exercise.
Habituate yourself to walk very far."

—Thomas Jefferson

3

GETTING TRAIL-READY

Now that you've arranged your time off, gathered your gear, and found a place to call home for a few days on the trail, it's time to go. Take a deep breath and relax. With some simple preparation, you'll be ready to take off into the wilds.

In this chapter, you'll learn what info to gather, a bit about navigation, some ideas for getting in trail shape, how to pack your gear, and some tips on techniques and setup you should know before you head out on the trail.

Gather Your Info

Before your big adventure, gather all the relevant information. Discovering at the trailhead that you forgot to pack the map is not only maddening, but it could also be the end of a meticulously planned weekend. Make your mom happy: Don't wander the wilderness without a map or if you forget your permit, driving directions, or other vital pieces of information.

What information should you gather before you hit the trail? Check this list, and then double-check it right before you go.

Print out your permits or know where to get your permits. Some land agencies will email your permit to you. Print it out and keep it in a handy place. Different organizations might direct you to the backcountry office to obtain the permit in person. Make the land agency's office your first destination once you reach the backcountry.

Carry a copy of any route info, historical tidbits, or guidebook information you've found from earlier research. A map is the primary means of navigation, but written material or an electronic map on your phone can assist in understanding an area, too.

Know the directions to the park, trailhead, and other important places. Since cell reception is spotty in many wilderness areas, bring a printed copy of the directions to the trailhead. Mapping software is not always accurate for backcountry areas. Verify the directions especially if the trailhead is in a place more obscure than a state or national park.

"Have map, will travel." Don't forget the map. Even with a GPS or GPS-enabled device, you need a print map of the backcountry to navigate safely.

Learn Navigation Skills

A modern adventurer should know how to navigate. Navigation can be as simple as knowing how to find your trails and campsites on a map or as complex as planning an off-trail route to Lake Shangri-La. However, the basics of navigation need not be difficult for your first backpacking journey. As your horizons expand to more complex and possibly off-trail travel, you'll want to find more in-depth materials about backcountry navigation and practice those concepts in the field. Refer to the appendix of this book on page 130 for information on resources to advance your backcountry navigational skills.

Beginning backpackers, however, need only master some basic concepts.

First, make sure you have an adequate map. It should be detailed enough that you can identify the correct trail, landmarks such as rivers or prominent mountains, and potential campsites. It should also cover enough area that you won't need to carry multiple maps.

National Geographic's "Trails Illustrated Maps" are a good, widely available option. They clearly identify trails, their medium scale represents a good compromise between overview and detail, and they typically list campsites, roads, and other useful points of interest. If you can procure one of these maps for an area, it usually means it's an excellent destination for your first trip.

These maps are available in outdoors stores, visitor centers, and online retailers. More obscure areas will require more logistics, planning, and possibly a more advanced skill set . . . but that's for a later trip.

Now that you have your map, let's see how to use it in the field. Learn how to read your map at home before heading out on your first trip.

First, look over the illustration details of the hiking map. You'll see marked trails, campsites, and other points of interest, including mountain peaks, rivers, overlooks, and other landscape features. It will also identify any backcountry offices in the area.

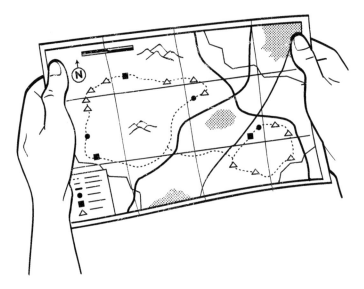

Now, take a close look at your compass.

First, notice the red magnetic arrow of the compass as shown in the illustration. Next, turn the bezel of the compass so both the direction of travel arrow and the north-orienting arrow align with the magnetic red arrow. This action is known as putting "Red Fred in the Shed," which means you've just lined up the compass so you are facing magnetic north. For other trips, you'll need to know true north versus magnetic north, but knowing magnetic north is enough to get started.

Now that you know where north is, take out your map, which is oriented on a north-south axis. Turn your map so that it's facing magnetic north. Look up with your map turned in the correct direction, and you should see where the trail leads,

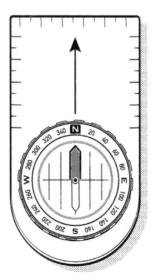

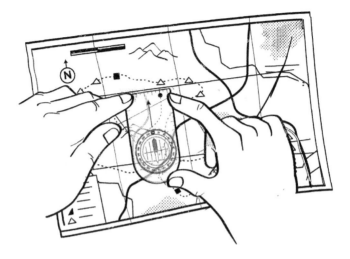

enabling you to navigate to your campsite or that spectacular lake you're looking for.

The resources listed on page 131 will help you learn more advanced concepts such as true north versus magnetic north, reading topographic lines, and even printing out custom maps. But the steps listed on the previous page should suffice for your first backpacking trip. And you'll continue using this method as you gain experience. When you're ready for more advanced trips, you'll probably want to take a class for more difficult backcountry navigation.

Finally, it should be noted that while phone maps and GPS make an excellent complement to practical mapping skills, you shouldn't rely them as your sole resource. Electronics can fail in wet or cold weather, run out of battery power, or even suffer from bugs and crashes. Furthermore, print maps provide a much broader overview than any five-inch screen.

Getting in Shape

As discussed in chapter 1 (page 3), if you are physically active in your daily life, your baseline physical health needs only a little tweaking in the weeks leading up to your first trip. Hiking and backpacking use different muscles and require different levels of endurance than activities like weight lifting, basketball, or even running. Continuing to perform your regular fitness routines is the best way to stay in shape. But in the four or five weeks before your first backpacking trip, incorporate hiking into your weekly schedule. On a weekend day, take an extended hike of about four hours in a hilly area with the gear and clothing you plan on using for your first backpacking adventure. Wear the exact shoes, socks, and loaded pack you're planning to use for your trip. Your body will get used to carrying weight, and you'll learn to adjust your gear as needed.

If you don't live in a hilly area, find a tall building and walk up and down the steps, use the stair stepper at the gym, or find some bleachers at a nearby school. Combine these stair workouts with regular walks on the flatter ground.

During the week, take a shorter walk or two (roughly an hour) with your gear. The exercise will help prepare you for backpacking, and it's an excellent way to decompress after a busy day at work.

If you are not physically active, start this routine two or three months before your first trip, depending on your overall fitness level. Start slow with mileage or time committed to the

PREPARING FOR STEEP CLIMBS

A steep climb up Lung Buster Pass can be intimidating for people new to the outdoors.

To prepare for steep climbs, work in steep climbs and hill training when possible. Climb steps if you're not in a hilly area. Be sure to train while wearing your gear. Gym workouts help build leg strength, but it's most important to walk; do it with your gear on steep terrain when you can.

The key to all of this, though, is to enjoy the climb. Find a pace that works for you. Don't work so hard that you're huffing and puffing, and take a break if you need to. Pause for a photo, sip some water, and enjoy the sunshine and the sound of birds.

hikes and walks. Before starting a fitness plan, always consult with a physician if you are not sure of your overall fitness level.

And have fun with your weekly hikes and walks. Listen to the birds sing or catch up on a favorite podcast. While you're preparing for your first backpacking trip, you'll also be giving yourself the gift of time in your daily life.

What to Practice

Unless you're Mary Poppins, things rarely go perfectly— remember our friend Murphy from chapter 1 (page 12)?

Practice will help you become familiar with your gear so that when Murphy does show up, you're ready. With practice, you'll enjoy your time in nature rather than fretting over every little thing that goes wrong or using words not suitable for family consumption. Here are a few skills to practice before you go:

Setting up your tent. In your backyard, the common area of your apartment complex, or a local park, learn how to set up your shelter quickly. It's usually not intuitive, so be sure to read the instructions. You'll learn the nuances of your shelter and be less frazzled if you have to set it up in rain or darkness on your trip.

Using your stove and cookset. A practical and easy way to get used to your stove and cookset is to boil some water at home for tea or hot chocolate. After a few more backpacking trips, use your stove at home to try out new backcountry recipes.

Carrying and adjusting your pack. With the physical conditioning plan in the previous section (page 53), you'll adjust the

HOW TO SURVIVE
ASSEMBLING YOUR TENT

Tents are marvelous pieces of gear that shelter you from the wind and rain, dry quickly, and pack efficiently—all in a package five pounds or less. So why do some of them seem like they require a degree in mechanical engineering to set up? No two tents assemble the same way, and the process is rarely intuitive. But by learning a few tips and tricks, it will be as simple as tying your shoe.

- Getting practice assembling your tent in a less challenging environment will make it easier when you get to camp.

- When you get to the campsite, clear away any rocks, pine cones, or other debris that may cause discomfort during sleep.

- Many tents should be staked first before you set up the poles. With this technique, you'll get a more stable and weather-resistant pitch. Again, be sure to follow your instructions.

- Don't zip up your tent completely. If weather allows, keep the doors and windows open a bit and let the air circulate. The human body breathes out up to two pints of moisture a night. If the tent is entirely zipped up, condensation will build up. Morning mist with sunlight coming through the trees may be lovely, but water dripping in your structure is not.

pack as needed. We'll discuss how to pack your gear effectively in the next section.

Trying out your hiking poles. Get in the habit of using them on your training hikes, and learn to adjust them as needed.

How to Pack

There are different ways to pack your gear. The shape of the pack, the weight of your equipment, and even the particular form and bulk of any given item can change how you pack your gear.

Luckily, backpacking is less gear-intense than other outdoor activities such as climbing, skiing, or car camping. You won't be packing a cooler, grill, or much extra sports gear. Backpacking is all about simplicity, and packing for a trip should follow suit.

First, line your pack with a large trash bag or, even better, a trash compactor bag. Not only are plastic liner bags cheaper than a pack cover, they are more waterproof and practical. They won't get snagged on branches, either. Pack covers are unnecessary because modern pack fabrics dry out quickly. But faster drying doesn't mean waterproof, so you'll need to use a pack liner to keep your clothing, sleeping bag, and other items from getting wet.

Then, load your shelter, accessories, sleeping bag, and pad into the bottom of the pack. External frame packs are less common days, but if you happen to have one, lash the sleeping bag to the bottom of the frame and the tent to the top.

On top of this layer, nestle your stove and fuel canister together in the cook pot. If you are using liquid fuel, place the container upright in a pocket outside the pack. Try on your pack to make sure these items don't poke you in the back.

Next, add your food bag or bear canister, tucking them on top of, or next to, the stove.

At the top of your pack, keep the following items so they are easily accessible: First-aid kit, rain gear, snacks for the day, warm layers of clothing, toilet paper, hand sanitizer, and potty trowel. You can also place these items in a lid or outside pocket on your pack.

Finally, place your water bottles in the holsters or, if using a bladder, in the appropriate pouch. Try on the pack to see how it fits; walk around a bit, and make adjustments as needed.

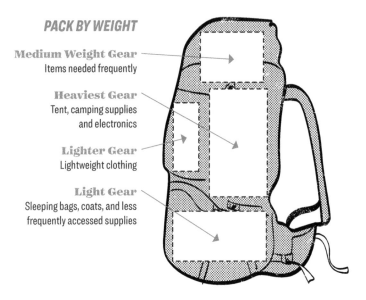

PACK BY WEIGHT

Medium Weight Gear
Items needed frequently

Heaviest Gear
Tent, camping supplies and electronics

Lighter Gear
Lightweight clothing

Light Gear
Sleeping bags, coats, and less frequently accessed supplies

HOW TO SURVIVE
UNEXPECTED WEATHER

If you follow the First Trip Checklist in the appendix (page 125), you should be prepared for most weather events, short of a hurricane or a blizzard. But there are some tips you can follow to get ready for unexpected weather.

First, don't take unnecessary chances. If there's a blizzard, hurricane, or another extreme weather event in the forecast, it's better to cancel your trip than to put yourself and others in danger.

If the weather is just a bit colder or wetter than expected, be prepared to get wet or to make use of your cold weather gear. Hands getting cold? Don't hesitate to put on your gloves and hat. Don't overdress, either. It's better to hike cool (not cold) than to overheat and sweat, which will cause you to catch a chill when you stop.

If it rains, take the same approach as dressing for cold. Throw on your rain jacket at the first sign of consistent rain. You'll also want to vent and adjust your zippers to avoid overheating.

One more tip: Always have a sacred stash of dry socks that will only be worn in camp. A couple pairs of warm, dry socks will not only warm you up in camp, but that coziness will give you a psychological boost, allowing you to enjoy the trip despite the weather.

If you can, wear your filled pack when training for your hike. Again, you'll not only get in shape for the trail, but you'll also see how your gear fits and works with your body before you take your first step into the woods.

As for your pocket knife, map, and compass, carry them in a clothing pocket. And only bring the bare necessities in your wallet: cash, credit cards, health insurance card, and maybe auto club information. You won't need your gym membership or library card in the backcountry.

Final Trip Checklist

Now that you've done all the right prep work, it's time to make sure you have all your gear, permits, logistics, and "just in case" items.

One week before the trip:

❑ Print permits, or find out where to get permits at the backcountry office.

❑ Print the directions to the trailhead.

❑ Arrange carpool info with trip partners. Decide who is driving, where to meet and at what time, and whether to stop for coffee, breakfast, or other items on the way to the trailhead.

❑ Figure out how to split up the gear, if necessary. Who will carry the tent poles and stakes, for example?

❑ Purchase food and supplies before the trip. Avoid buying supplies the night before a trip. It's hectic to be running around on a Friday night trying to get ready, and you are more likely to forget something. Imagine the horror of backpacking without chocolate and coffee!

❏ Share the trip plan with family or friends. In addition to the basic location and dates of your trip, let them know your itinerary, including planned campsites and trail routes. Be sure to list contact info for the park or land management agency, as well as phone numbers for anyone in your party who's bringing a phone. Instruct your family or friends to notify the land management agency if they don't hear from you within 24 hours after your expected return.

Two days before leaving:

❏ Pack your gear. Again, don't wait until the night before you leave.

One day before:

❏ Check in with your trip partners. Is everyone ready? Are there any hiccups to be aware of before leaving?

❏ Charge up electronics. Take a backup battery if you anticipate heavy use.

❏ Do a last-minute weather check. While you can probably handle a little rain or cooler-than-expected temperatures, if the forecast calls for the Hurricane of the Century over the weekend, you may need to reschedule the trip.

❏ Stage your gear for departure. Put your pack and hiking poles together. Lay out your clothes for the first day's hike.

❏ Refrain from drinking too much alcohol or eating spicy foods that might upset your stomach.

❏ Set your alarm, and get a good night's sleep. You are prepared, relaxed, and organized. You'll do great.

"It's pretty far, but it doesn't seem like it."

—Yogi Berra

4

HITTING THE TRAIL

This is where the hiking shoe meets the trail. You probably feel excited, and maybe a touch nervous. But don't worry: If you can survive the planning, shopping, and physical preparation, you'll definitely survive the trail itself.

In this chapter, you'll learn about proper hiking form, the dos and don'ts of trail etiquette, and how to navigate your surroundings. And when Murphy inevitably rears his pesky head again, you'll learn how to calmly handle the situation.

Proper Hiking Form

Most of us become proficient at walking around the age of four, and it's something we do often for the rest of our lives. Bruce Springsteen may have said that we were "born to run," but we're even better adapted for walking.

Though hiking is a bit more involved than taking a stroll in your local park, it doesn't have to be difficult. Following a few core concepts will help make your first backcountry hike a joy rather than a trudge.

Find a good pace and form. Your ideal pace is one you can maintain consistently. Follow the Goldilocks principle: not too fast, not too slow, but just right. Your level of fitness, the terrain type, the steepness of the trail, and even your mood will affect your pace. Try to maintain a "conversational" pace; if you're not able to converse while hiking, you're going too fast. Slow down a bit. You'll sustain energy for the day, enabling you to make it over that next hill. When walking, pay attention to your form. Take longer strides on flat ground and shorter strides when heading up or downhill. When hiking more challenging terrain with a lot of rocks, roots, or uneven ground, pay attention to where you step so that you don't trip or roll an ankle.

Adjust your shoes. Your laces shouldn't be so tight that your feet ache or so loose that they slide around in your shoe. A proper fit makes hiking easier on various types of terrain and helps decrease muscle fatigue. If a pebble or other debris works its way into your shoe, don't try to tough it out. Stop for a moment to remove the debris before moving on. Debris in the shoe can cause blisters to develop, and, as most backcountry veterans can attest, that's not a fun way to hike.

Fit your pack properly. Distribute the gear correctly in your pack as discussed in chapter 3 (page 57). Efficient distribution of gear will make your pack more comfortable to carry, cause less stress and fatigue on the upper body, and provide easier access to packed items. Once you pack the gear correctly, make adjustments to the pack itself. Modern packs are designed to make it easy to adjust the amount of weight placed on your hips and shoulders. Adjust so the weight does not feel too heavy on your shoulders or hips. Depending on your physique, preferences, and musculature, the ratio of pressure for hips to the shoulders will vary. Fit the pack so that it feels comfortable. As you keep hiking, you may find other adjustments necessary.

Snack regularly. Hiking burns calories, which mean you'll need fuel. Rather than a long lunch stop, take frequent (once an hour, ideally) snack breaks. Having food in a convenient pocket helps keep your system running and enables you to maintain a consistent pace. Trail mix, granola bars, jerky, and other salty snacks make excellent trail food.

Stay hydrated. Sip water often, but don't gulp. Some hikers like to add drink mixes, but the typical hiker's diet has enough electrolytes and salts without them. Remember, you should be drinking at least one liter of water for every five miles you hike.

Stop to rest every 2 or 3 hours. Breaks of no more than 15 minutes prevent muscles from stiffening while still allowing your body to rest. As you gain more experience, you can calibrate the number of breaks you need for your hiking style. Take a photo, stretch, eat some chocolate, and sip water. Be sure to enjoy the view.

Try to avoid poison oak or poison ivy. You'll spot it using the old adage "Leaves of three, leave 'em be." If you accidentally touch your skin to these plants, clean the area with your hand sanitizer applied by a bandana, and then rinse the area with water. Further treatment might be necessary at home for more severe cases.

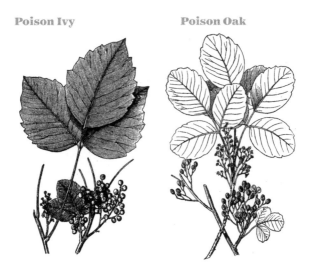

Poison Ivy

Poison Oak

Trail Etiquette

Trail etiquette is not a set of rules, but rather practices that create pleasant interactions with others on the trail. Here are some backcountry etiquette principles to follow:

Be courteous of other hikers. Try not to speak loudly when others are nearby. If you are listening to music while hiking, use earbuds. Many hikers will wear just one earbud so they are more aware of their surroundings.

Take a break on the side of the trail, not on it. Don't block the path for other hikers.

Leave no trace. Refer back to the rules you learned on page 13. Even organic food waste like apple cores should be packed out.

Be courteous of other people at high use areas such as mountain summits. Don't hog the summit or viewpoint for your selfies.

Keep any dogs on-leash if required (or under voice control if not). Pack out all dog waste, and abide all regulations about pets. The rules might be there to protect local wildlife.

Don't feed the wildlife. Despite what friendly cartoon bears might say, habituated animals lose their ability to thrive in the wild.

Don't take shortcuts on switchbacks. Though it may be tempting to take a shortcut to the next portion of a trail below a switchback, don't do it. You'll cause erosion and ruin trail conditions for others.

Leave only footprints and take only photos. Don't pick the wildflowers or grab rocks or cultural artifacts to take home.

When you've got to go, do it 200 feet away. When going to the bathroom, stay 200 feet away from the trail and 200 feet away from any water sources. In some areas, the land agency requires that you pack out your toilet paper. Chapter 6 (page 87) will cover potty break procedure in more detail.

If you need to use a mobile device, treat it like going to the bathroom. If you need to make a call, step out of sight, use a low voice, and be respectful other wilderness users and their experience.

Remember, other groups are sharing the trail with you. Hikers yield to horses and should either move off to the far side of the trail or step off on the downhill side of the horse. If you're in a group, step aside to make it easier for a solo traveler or smaller group to get around you. And if your group's pace is slower than another person or group, step aside and let them pass.

You'll often find that the best thing to do is situational, such as allowing a person to pass up and downhill. Saying "please" and "thank you," giving a friendly smile, and even a quick "hello" can make life on the trail more enjoyable for everyone.

HOW TO SURVIVE
A LIGHTNING STORM

Lightning can be scary in the backcountry, especially while out on an exposed trail, but by following some basic safety measures, you can minimize risk.

Look out for large clouds. If you see large, dark clouds building up, don't head toward them. The best way to avoid lightning danger is to avoid exposing yourself to it in the first place.

If you are above the tree line, head down to the trees. Lightning typically strikes high points, so move away from areas where you're the tallest target around. That said, don't stand next to the tallest tree in an open area either.

Don't stand in an open field. Again, don't make yourself the highest point in the area.

Use the "lightning crouch." Crouch down on your heels and hold your hands behind your neck to make yourself small. While there is debate about the effectiveness of this technique, it can't hurt.

Spread out if you're in a group. A larger target is more susceptible to lightning strikes, so spreading out your group minimizes risk. If the worst happens and someone gets hit, have one person provide first aid while another goes for help (if you don't have cell-phone service).

Following the Trail

Following a beginner-friendly trail is not tricky. These trails are typically well-marked and -maintained, and they usually have obvious tread. If you pick one of the trails in the appendix of this book (see Trips for First-Time Backpackers on page 115), you'll find a path that's appropriate for your first trip in the wilderness.

While there is no uniform method for marking trails, there are common markers found on typical backcountry trails:

Trail signs are very self-explanatory. Located at trailheads and trail junctions, these signs point out the direction to lakes or indicate trail splits, campsites, trailhead parking lots, and other features.

Blazes are roughly two-by-six-inch painted rectangles found on trees, rocks, or even fence posts. Follow the blazes and you'll follow the trails. Blazes are very common in trails east of the Mississippi River. The Appalachian Trail's white blazes are quite possibly the most famous blazes of them all.

Carsonite posts are often found in the desert or similar environments. These plastic composite markers are about four to five feet high and often marked with trail insignia or trail number designations.

Cairn is an old Scottish term that means "pile of rocks." You'll see this type of trail marking on rocky terrain such as slickrock in canyon country or alpine areas located on higher mountains.

Even with trail markings, consult your navigation aids. It's easy to miss a turn if you're not paying attention. If you think that's happened, orient your map as we discussed in the previous chapter (page 51). Check to see if the terrain and other landmarks line up with your current location. If not, pause and backtrack a bit. If you catch a misstep early, you'll avoid a major crisis.

As mentioned before (page 52), phone maps or GPS make an excellent complement to traditional navigational aids like a print map and compass. But they're not without faults. While a mobile device will assist in finding the trail on a large, macro scale, it rarely helps with finer, micro-level navigation.

Micro-level navigation means being able to follow the twists and turns of a trail through the woods, or spotting a cairn in a sea of nearly identical-looking rocks on a foggy day.

GETTING LOST

What if you lose the trail? Zigged where you should have zagged? In the words of the classic book, *The Hitchhiker's Guide to the Galaxy*, "Don't panic."

Instead, pause and look around. Did you step over a log that indicated a closure? Maybe you missed a cairn and walked down a dry stream bed that looked like an old trail? Try backtracking to the place you last remember. Some trail signs may be overgrown and easy to miss, especially if you're distracted.

If you're still lost, use the **STOP** methodology as advised by government agencies.

Stop. When you realize you are lost, pause and take a deep breath. Remember, don't panic.

Think. Consult your map and your GPS. Does the terrain match your map? Do you recognize landmarks? Does your GPS display your location? Don't move until you've planned your next step.

Observe. Look around. Backtracking is typically the best course of action. You'll eventually come to another trail junction with signs that match with your maps. If you went off-trail by accident, go back to the "Think" stage and use your compass to hike in a direction that will take you back to a trail.

Plan. Put the previous steps into action. Be sure the goal is realistic and within your physical capabilities; planning to hike another 10 miles an hour before sunset may not be practical. A good night's rest in an emergency camp will leave you physically and mentally refreshed and able to hike out with confidence the following day.

CROSSING A CREEK

Crossing a stream can be tricky. The current may be swift, and unsure footing on slick rocks can lead to a fall. Since this is your first trip, be conservative. Follow trails with maintained bridges where streams are rarely above your knees. Check the appendix for route ideas (page 115).

Follow these steps to safely cross a stream:

First, place anything that can't get wet—camera, phone, key fob, etc.—securely in your pack (even a brief dunk in the water can quickly destroy expensive electronics).

Second, never cross barefoot. Regular trail shoes are best. Once you've crossed the stream, switch into dry socks.

Next, look for shallow rapids over visible rocks. Still waters are typically deep and often contain swirling currents of water called eddies that can easily knock you over.

To cross, angle upstream, walking against the current. Use hiking poles to steady yourself and to probe ahead while walking.

If there is an official closure due to a rockslide, flooding, or other event, the trailhead kiosk will list alternate routes available to you. If the trail is blocked due to blowdowns (trees blown over in a wind storm) or a rockslide and there is no official alternate, assess the area. Some small blowdowns are easy enough to walk over and around. But if the area does not seem safe or there is no way to walk around, read your map. If there's another trail nearby that could provide an alternate route, follow that trail. And continue with the joy of walking.

Taking a Dog on the Trail

Taking a dog on a backpacking trip seems natural to many. Hiking with your faithful friend is a pleasing image, but it's best to temper this romantic notion with a dose of reality.

For your first trip, leave Sierra, Dakota, or Cuddles at home. Get your trail legs before you deal with the logistics of taking a dog. Dogs require additional planning. Almost all national parks do not allow dogs, which limits your destination options. Also, consider leash laws. Is your dog comfortable on a leash all day? If leashes aren't mandated, does your companion have excellent obedience to voice control and training? Other hikers won't appreciate it if Fido is less trained than you initially thought.

Hiking with a dog requires the proper gear and training, and you have to pick places that are a good fit for your dog's health and age. Refer to some of the resources at the back of this book (page 131) for more information about backpacking with your pup.

AVOIDING CRYPTOBIOTIC SOIL

"Take only photos and leave only footprints" is a mantra that's often repeated on the trail. The only trace you should leave behind are footprints.

There is, however, one major exception to this rule: cryptobiotic soil.

Also known as living soil crust or biological soil, cryptobiotic soil is found throughout the Southwest desert. This living crust, which is similar to lichen, holds the desert soil together and helps prevent erosion in one of the most fragile ecosystems in the United States. It stores water for other desert plants and provides nitrogen for plant growth.

Cryptobiotic soil takes years or even decades to grow. But one careless footprint can destroy the plant. It grows in piles on the desert floor, and you can recognize it by its distinct black, knobby appearance.

When in terrain with biological soil, stay on the trail. Don't leave footprints behind and "don't bust the crust."

"My tent doesn't look like much but, as an estate agent might say, 'It is air-conditioned and has exceptional location.'"

—Fennel Hudson

5

SETTING UP CAMP

Congratulations! You've survived your first day on the trail and are now ready for some well-earned rest and relaxation. First, though, you've got to set up camp. You'll need to find a campsite (if you haven't already selected one before the trip), pick the perfect spot for your tent, and prepare the area to ensure a safe, enjoyable evening.

Give yourself about an hour to set up camp for your first few times out. While the steps aren't complicated, they're not intuitive to most first-time backpackers. When planning for your trip, note the sunset times, and make sure your pace gets you into camp on time. You should have a rough idea of how fast you walk per mile based on your practice hikes.

And while giving yourself one hour to set up camp may be effective, you might want more camp time to fish, birdwatch, take photographs, or just relax. You've hiked all day, climbed mountains, and put in a good sweat. Make a comfortable camp; you deserve it.

The Five Steps to Setting Up Camp

Setting up camp is not tricky. You don't need the wood savvy of Davy Crockett or the "can-do" skills of MacGyver. Here are a few easy steps to set up for a hot meal, a comfortable sleep, and an easy pack up in the morning.

1. **Take a quick snack break.** As any good Italian grandmother would say, "*Mangia!*" You have been walking all day, and your body needs fuel to stay warm. Before setting up a shelter, eat a quick snack such as a handful of trail mix, and take a sip of water.

2. **Change into your thermal layers, a warm hat, and your fleece or puffy as needed.** Keeping your body warm is easier than fighting the cold. So, putting on warm layers early will save you the hassle of trying to warm up your cold body later. You need to retain heat, and your body cools down fast once you stop moving.

3. **Set up your shelter.** You've practiced this, so setup should be a breeze. Be mindful of other parties in a shared campsite. If you can, set up out of sight from other parties or at least far enough way so your conversations do not disturb them. And don't set up so close to your trip partners that you impose on their privacy. Double-check the list in the back of this book (page 125) to make sure you don't forget any parts of your tent.

4. **Get your bed ready for the evening.** Set up your sleeping pad, take out and fluff your sleeping bag, and put your

headlamp in a convenient place so you won't have to grope around for it at night. Please, no mints on the pillow. You'll find out why in the next chapter (page 87).

5. **Set up your kitchen.** Find an appropriate place to set up where you and your friends will cook dinner. We'll discuss this step in more details on page 85.

Finalizing Your Campsite

While you likely picked a campsite using the methods discussed in chapter 1 (page 7), you may need to fine-tune your campsite selection once you get there.

Look for a flat area free of plants that has a durable surface like sand or pine duff. It's ideal if this area is also surrounded by trees, which will help buffer the wind and maintain a little warmth. Areas with trees often have ground cover that makes sleeping more comfortable and adds R-value to your sleeping pad.

What are some other amenities to look for when fine-tuning the campsite? Perhaps you want to set up your shelter so the sunrise greets you in the morning. Or, maybe you'd like the sound of a nearby creek to lull you to sleep. When available, pick the campsite that is good for you.

Preventing a Tent Malfunction

While equipment can fail, using proper setup techniques can minimize potential mishaps in the field. Though you practiced setting up your shelter at home, the practical backcountry

SETTING UP A TENT ON A SLOPE

So, what should you do if you get to the site you reserved weeks ago only to find that the ground is uneven, and you're forced to pitch your tent at a slight angle?

Set up your shelter perpendicular to the slope. With one side of the tent lower than the other, you won't be sliding up or down all night. Use your extra clothes or your pack to level the sleeping pad on one side. In essence, construct a makeshift shim.

Still can't even out your sleeping position? Sleep with your head higher than your feet. This tends to be more comfortable.

application will be a little different. The ground might be harder, the wind stronger, and you'll probably be more tired.

Follow these steps to help make sure you set up the tent correctly:

Be sure to have a taut pitch. This means the fabric of the shelter is stretched tightly so that it sheds rain and wind easier. You'll have a more weatherproof tent and a more comfortable night's sleep.

Even behind a shelter of trees, pitch your tent so the narrowest part of the shelter faces the wind. A smaller surface area means the tent is less likely to be buffeted by the wind and make noise all evening. This puts less stress on the tent's rainfly and stakes, too.

Speaking of tent stakes, always stake down your tent. Winds can pick up even on calm nights, and I've seen more than one tent turn into a giant sail. Place the stakes into the ground facing the tent at a 45-degree angle; stakes at this angle will have more holding power than stakes placed away from the tent or at a 90-degree angle. Remember, even a freestanding tent needs to be staked down.

And if you forget tent stakes or the tent poles? You'll be all right; relax and improvise. Tie the tent loops to branches or rocks, for example. Or, use some sticks as makeshift tent poles. Be creative. What around you can be substituted for what you left at home? Maybe you'll be a backcountry MacGyver after all!

TENT STAKES IN HARD GROUND

The backcountry is as varied as you'd imagine, and sometimes you'll encounter soil that's as hard as rock. This can make staking your tent a Herculean task. Here's how to do it without bending your equipment, bruising a finger, or yelling unsportsmanlike words:

Pour a small amount of water where you plan to place a tent stake. Wait a minute or two for water to settle. Then, place the stake and use a BAR (big ample rock) to gently tap in the stake (only use your foot if the ground is soft enough). Repeat this process until you've placed all the stakes.

Setting Up for Cooking

Setting up the kitchen in your campsite begins with finding a central spot where everyone can gather. In the established sites suggested for first-time backpackers, there are designated eating spots at least 200 feet away from water and your tents. Many of these established sites have a picnic table. If you are using a dispersed site, use the same concepts. The Leave No Trace principles advocate camping, cooking, and cleaning away from water. Cooking away from your shelter is good practice as well; you don't want strong food odors in your sleeping area.

Once you've chosen the appropriate place for a camp kitchen, look for a large flat rock or something similar where you can stage your stove, cooking pot, and cooking utensils. Use a picnic table if there's one on the site. Have plenty of water near the stove; you'll need it to cook your meals, clean up, and make any beverages.

Other features to consider when choosing your kitchen site are large logs to sit on; natural windbreaks such as bushes, boulders, or thicker stands of trees; and pleasant views to enjoy while cooking and eating. You'll typically spend much of your camp time in the kitchen area, so make sure it's both in an efficient and comfortable location.

"A near tragedy: the first week out on the expedition someone lost the bottle opener, and for the rest of the trip we had to subsist on food and water."

—W. C. Fields

6

COOKING AND CAMP LIFE

Most backpackers eagerly look forward to camp time. It offers a chance to relax, eat, and sleep after a day of invigorating exercise, steep climbs, and fresh air.

In this chapter, you'll learn how to cook efficiently in camp. You'll also learn more about campfires (and why you may want to skip one), proper bathroom etiquette, and how to survive an encounter with "da bears."

Cooking Basics

You don't need to be Julia Child to master the art of back-packing cooking. Most meals on the trail are of the "boil water, add food, and eat" variety. That doesn't mean you can't get more elaborate, but it's best to keep it simple. Make some of the meals discussed earlier in the book, and save the gourmet delights for later trips.

The basics of cooking in camp can be broken down into a few steps:

Learn to use your stove. There are many different models and types of stoves. As discussed earlier in the book (page 34), you should read your stove's manual and practice using the equipment before you head out on the trail. For the canister stoves suggested for first-time use: simply screw the stove into the fuel canister directly; next, partially turn the gas knob, and then light the stove. Most canister stoves have an adjustable flame that allows you to set the flame at simmer, high heat, and anything in between.

Boil the water for a meal. Most backpacking meals require two cups of water. For freeze-dried pouch meals, add two cups of water to the pot, and place the pot on the stove. If you plan to make a hot drink, add another cup of water. Set the flame to a medium-low setting to conserve fuel. You'll only need the water to come to a low, not rolling, boil. Stoves are quieter at a lower heat, too. Once the water is boiling, prepare food and beverages per directions on the packaging.

Clean up the dishes as discussed earlier in the book (page 35). Use water with no soap for cleaning, and scrape out any food particles to pack out. You'll need to pack out your leftovers, too. Do not bury or disperse any leftover food; this will attract animals and habituate them to human presence. That said, if you've hiked all day, you probably won't have any leftovers.

Protecting Your Food from Wildlife

Although bears are a big concern for many new backpackers, especially when it comes to food, critters such as squirrels, chipmunks, mice, porcupines, and even deer are more likely to be an issue.

You may have heard about bear bagging—the practice of hoisting your food in a tree. But the reality is it's an increasingly antiquated practice that's sometimes not even allowed in dense bear activity areas. Some backcountry sites have a pole or even a metal bear locker to help you store your food.

If yours doesn't, here are some suggestions to avoid encounters with bears and other critters (always contact the land management agency to inquire as to the appropriate methods allowed in their jurisdiction):

Don't camp in popular areas if given the option. Animals are smart. They go where acquiring food is easy. See a broad, impacted area with a fire ring and trash? Don't camp there. Finding another site is not always an option, especially in a National Park Service campsite where the spot is designated. But try to avoid these heavily used sites if you can.

On a similar note, avoid camping where animals feed or linger. Stay away from huckleberry patches and watering holes. Mice are very likely to be present and will try to get into your food.

Use an odor-resistant bag like an Opsak, which mitigates the smell of food. These can be purchased at outdoor stores. Place these bags inside your bear canister or food storage bag. The food bags should not be placed inside your shelter.

A Kevlar bear bag is another option. The Ursack is the most popular of these items. You do not need to hang the bag; simply tie it around a tree trunk or something similar. The Interagency Grizzly Bear Committee (IGBC) certifies the Ursacks as both grizzly- and black bear–proof and a suitable alternative to the heavier and bulkier hard-sided bear canisters traditionally used. Unfortunately, though the IGBC certifies the Ursack as effective, not all land management agencies allow their use.

Lastly, a hard-sided bear canister is the easiest and arguably most effective critter and bear-resistant gear at this time. And they are increasingly mandated for use by land management agencies. A bear canister is a hard, plastic container with a screw top that can only be opened with opposable thumbs by twisting the cover on and off. Though failures do happen with canisters, they are more reliable than other methods. On the downside, a canister weighs as much as a day's worth of food (two pounds or more) and, because it is hard-sided plastic, does not fit well in backpacks. Still, the ease of use—and the fact that bear canisters are increasingly required—makes them an attractive option.

If none of these suggestions work, and you've got to string up a bear bag, read on to learn how.

The simplest method is to place your food in a stuff sack, attach the stuff sack to about 50 feet of cord, and tie the other end of the cord to a rock. Next, find a tree about 200 feet away from your campsite that has a thick branch about 15 feet above the ground and at least 10 feet from the tree trunk itself. Then tie a rock to the end of the cord and throw the rock over the branch. Pull down on the cord to raise the bear bag. Tie the end of the rope with the rock to the tree trunk.

AT LEAST
12 FEET ABOVE

AT LEAST
10 FEET AWAY

HOW TO SURVIVE
BEARS IN YOUR CAMP

While the likelihood of bear encounters is very low and much less of a risk than ticks, hypothermia, or even rolling your ankle, it's an issue that concerns many backpackers, experienced and new alike.

In the continental United States, grizzly bear encounters are not common; they're only found in a few pockets such as the Cascades of Washington, the Wind River Range in Wyoming, and parts of Montana, like Glacier National Park and Yellowstone. As a beginner, you shouldn't head into grizzly bear territory for your first backpacking trip. It provides extra stress (and equipment, like bear spray) that new backpackers should avoid.

Instead, let's talk about black bears, which are smaller and less aggressive than grizzlies. Black bears have become habituated to popular campsites, so they're more commonly encountered. What should you do if a black bear wanders into your camp?

First, stay calm. Getting excited might agitate the bear.

Don't run. It might trigger a chase instinct in a bear.

Talk in a low, calm voice. Then slowly back away without turning around, and avoid direct eye contact. As you are backing away, raise your arms overhead to look bigger.

If the bear makes a low huffing sound and otherwise acts aggressive, you are still too close. Continue to slowly back up.

If the black bear makes a bluff charge, hold your ground. Continue to keep your eyes on the ground and your arms raised.

Leave the bear a lot of space for an exit path. Always detour wide around the bear, too.

If the bear does not go away, yell or clap your hands. Making a lot of noise or throwing rocks toward (not at) the bear will help scare it away.

Bears are part of the wild. If you're lucky enough to encounter one, you'll be able to appreciate the experience by familiarizing yourself with these safety tips.

Note: If you're afraid of things like mountain lions or snakes showing up in your campsite, you needn't be.

Snakes are cold-blooded creatures that mostly come out during the warmth of the day. You might see a snake on a trail; if you do, give it a wide berth, especially if it hisses or rattles. Mountain lions are not interested in most adult humans, who are too big to be an easy meal. If you do see a mountain lion, use the same steps recommended for black bears.

And if you see Sasquatch? Take a good video on your phone, submit it to a news organization, and count your dough.

Campfires

In the popular imagination, campfires and backpacking go together like chocolate, marshmallows, and graham crackers. A person can almost conjure up the sound of the crackling logs, the smell of wood smoke, and the orange glow of embers on a cool summer evening in the mountains. But the reality of campfires in modern times is far different.

Frankly, campfires in the backcountry are going the way of burying garbage, cutting down pine boughs for bedding, and adding trenches around tents to prevent flooding. These formerly accepted backcountry practices are simply not in line with modern backcountry use.

In the more wildfire-prone areas of the American West, fires are often banned in the backcountry and are usually only allowed in the established fire rings at car camping sites. There are many reasons not to make a campfire in the backcountry:

Backcountry campfires are typically illegal in most land management areas. To put it simply, you can't create a campfire even when the conditions are not hot and dry. And speaking of hot and dry weather . . .

Almost every summer, various land agencies will ban campfires. Not only will there be a ban when wildfires are present, but many agencies are also increasingly issuing preemptive bans on campfires to prevent wildfires from occurring at all.

Gathering wood and building fire rings for campfires damages the local ecosystem. Decaying wood is a crucial component for healthy soil from which plant life grows, providing sustenance that works its way up the food chain. And all the people searching for wood creates worn trails where none had previously existed. These trails further harm the environment by damaging the soil, creating paths for water erosion, and ruining the aesthetics of a site. Additionally, a fire ring mars the landscape, and the fire itself creates dead soil where plants can no longer grow.

A backcountry campfire requires much work. If you're properly following the Leave No Trace principles, it's a lot of hard to work to keep a fire going and (most important) extinguish it before bedtime. You may need to gather gallons of water to have nearby. After a hard day of hiking, you're probably not going to be up for it.

Backcountry campfires can damage gear. Cooking on a campfire creates soot on pots and may weaken the metal on the light cookware that backpackers typically favor. Additionally, embers can melt nylon and other forms of synthetic clothing quickly and leave a permanent wood smoke smell in the fibers (unlike wool or cotton, synthetic fibers tend to retain odor longer).

Backcountry campfires are not efficient for warmth. Carrying thicker or additional layers will keep you warmer than a typical backcountry campfire.

Aesthetically, a campfire distracts you from enjoying the night sky. Sitting around a fire, you usually can't see all the stars, and the moonlit landscape disappears into the background.

Save campfires for established campsites in permitted areas of the front country, or for emergencies such as needing to dry out wet clothing or sleeping bags.

However, if you must have a backcountry campfire, be sure you adhere to these Leave No Trace principles and safety protocols:

Check with the land agency where you are backpacking. Call to get the most updated information; even the agency website might not reflect the most recent fire restrictions. If fires are not allowed, and you create one illegally, you risk a fine that can go into the hundreds of dollars. And if you cause a wildfire because of an illegal campfire, you could face penalties in the thousands of dollars.

Build your fires in existing fire rings only; do not create new ones. The ground is already damaged in these existing rings, and you will not cause further damage to the environment.

Next, gather downed wood only. Don't collect wood from live trees or peel off the bark. Don't gather firewood in the area immediately around your campsite for the reasons discussed on pages 95 and 96. Gather wood at least 200 feet away from the campsite. Wood should be no larger than an adult's wrist, as all wood must be burnt down to ashes. Unburnt wood is unsightly and doesn't always get appropriately extinguished.

You will need to gather three types of wood: tinder, kindling, and logs. Tinder consists of pine needles, leaves, or small twigs. Kindling comprises small sticks about the size of an adult index finger. Logs will keep the fire burning through the night once the kindling catches fire with the tinder.

Keep the campfire small. A small campfire is not only easier to build and keep going for the evening but also uses fewer resources and has less impact on the environment.

Clean out any debris around the campfire ring. Any leaves, pine needles, twigs, or other easily flammable material near a fire can quickly ignite and turn into an uncontrolled burn. You'll need at least a six-foot radius of bare dirt around the campfire.

Grab at least one gallon of water to put out a campfire or accidental wildfires. It's much safer to have the water handy rather than frantically scrambling to find it should you face an emergency.

There are a few different ways to build a campfire, but the classic tipi fire is the simplest overall for beginners. Make a small pile of tinder, and then stack the kindling in a tipi or cone shape over the tinder. Don't bunch up the kindling so tight that oxygen can't freely move; you need air circulation to form an effective fire. When the kindling ignites, gradually add the firewood logs, stacking them tipi-style and leaving enough room between the kindling so air circulates freely.

Light the tinder. Use a lighter to ignite the tinder while gently blowing on the base of the fire. This provides circulation and creates a more intense fire to light the kindling.

Once the kindling has a steady flame, gradually add logs as described above.

Don't burn trash in the campfire. Burning trash releases toxins into the air, and it rarely burns up completely.

Remember that fire is dangerous; be safe! Sit far enough away from the fire so that stray embers won't ignite or melt clothing. Use a stick to turn the logs throughout the evening. Finally, never, ever, leave a campfire unattended. A stray ember can ignite a wildfire quickly.

Before going to bed for the evening, extinguish your campfire. Pour ample water on the fire to extinguish it;

stir the ashes, and then apply more water. Repeat this cycle until the ashes are cool to the touch and the campfire is extinguished completely.

Campfires do provide a warm and welcoming glow for many people. But if you're looking for an alternative that requires much less work and risk, there are many inexpensive inflatable and solar-charged lanterns that are compact and weigh roughly four ounces. Better yet, look at the stars above and revel in the beauty of the night sky, free of city lights. You might see the Milky Way, shooting stars, and other wonders not usually visible due to light pollution.

Camp Etiquette

Whether you're sharing a campsite with friends or you're camped near another party, proper etiquette helps make the backcountry pleasant for everyone.

If you're up after dark, keep your conversations low. People need sleep when backpacking, so be considerate.

If you are an early riser, don't make too much noise when cooking or packing up. This is especially important at a shared campsite or shelter such as those found on the Appalachian Trail.

Use headphones when listening to music in camp. Not everyone wants to listen to your music. Save it for the club.

Be mindful of mobile device etiquette. If you have reception and must make a phone call, walk away from the camp.

Your fellow campers likely don't want to listen to a lengthy conversation about the family pet, Mr. Cuddles.

Use the headlamps on low-light or even red-light mode if available. A bright light shined in someone's eyes can affect how well they see at night or even wake someone up if pointed at a tent.

Go to the bathroom before going to bed. Admittedly, sometimes you've just got to go in the middle of the night. But relieving yourself before going to sleep decreases the likelihood.

Bathing and Hygiene

Although a little dirt will always be part of the backpacking experience, there's no reason to be filthy. Proper hygiene will make you feel better, help prevent the spread of illness, and even make your gear last longer.

You don't need special gear for basic hygiene. Pack an extra bandana or even a cheap dish sponge for washing, a one-gallon resealable freezer bag to hold water for cleaning, some hand sanitizer, and a potty trowel for bathroom use. Some people bring baby wipes, but that's extra garbage that you'll need to pack out. If you use soap (even if biodegradable), don't rinse off in a lake, stream, or river.

Follow proper bathroom etiquette. In a shared campsite, don't urinate where people eat or sleep. If there is no outhouse, you will need to be at least 200 feet from camp for bowel movements. Use your trowel to dig a cat hole (a 6-inch-deep hole).

Defecate into the hole, and once you are done and finished wiping, cover up the hole with the dirt you dug. Note that in high-use, sensitive areas like Utah's national parks, you'll be required to pack out your toilet paper. Don't worry; it's not as bad as it sounds. For short backpacking trips, carry two resealable freezer bags and a plastic shopping bag to carry them in. Don't burn your toilet paper.

Avoid "monkey butt." This is a nasty, itchy rash where you don't want it. You can prevent it by cleaning yourself nightly and always after going No. 2. In hot, humid weather, a clean backside is especially important, and toilet paper alone won't do the trick. Jock itch can also be a problem. Get rid of those salts, and rinse off your undershorts (away from water, please). Some find hiking with baggy shorts and no underwear to be effective because of the increased ventilation.

Keep hands clean to prevent gastrointestinal illnesses. Use hand sanitizer after going No. 2 and before a shared meal to keep everyone healthy.

Don't forget to brush and floss. Brush your teeth away from natural water sources and where people eat and sleep. Don't spit large portions of toothpaste on the ground or you'll attract animals. Instead, use water to swish the toothpaste in your mouth before spitting. You'll need to pack out any used floss.

Avoid the "agony of da feet." Grit in your shoes and around your feet causes blisters, and wearing sweaty socks too long leads to athlete's foot. Rinse your feet off with a sponge or spare bandana, and rinse out your socks, too. Then, let your feet dry out before putting on clean socks. Attach wet socks to the back of your pack the next day to dry them.

Rinse off salt and sweat. Salt caused by sweating can lead to chafing, especially after many hours of hiking. To avoid a rash between your thighs or anywhere else that rubs, wipe them down with a bandana to get rid of the sweat salt.

Clean the upper body, and you'll feel better. Rinse your face, pits, and scalp (if bald) to help mitigate oils and bacteria that cause odor, acne, or even boils. Wash your face before bed to prevent problematic skin conditions.

Dealing with that time of the month. If your trip falls during menstruation, many experienced backpackers advise using a menstrual cup instead of paper products that will need to be packed out. Try using the cup a few times before your trip to make sure it works for you. To empty the cup, dig a cat hole as you would to go No. 2, rinse, and wipe the cup clean with toilet paper. If you decide to stick with paper products, pack out all waste as you would toilet paper—in a doubled-up zip-top freezer bag.

Basic hygiene extends the life of your gear and clothing. All the sweat, oil, and salt cause wear and tear on sleeping bags and down jackets. The insulation will be less effective as the loft of the sleeping bag decreases. Wash up before going to bed to keep your sleeping bag in better condition.

HOW TO SURVIVE
ALTERNATIVES TO TOILET PAPER

Of course, if you're completely put off by the idea of packing out TP (or if you forgot to bring it), there are options for paperless hygiene.

Grasses or large leaves work well. Place the plants you've used in the cat hole. Remember not to use plants like poison ivy—"leaves of three, leave 'em be."

Snow works too. You need to be able to make a snowball; non-compacted dry snow won't do the trick. This method is most effective with early summer snow that lingers in the mountains.

Many women use a dedicated bandana as a "pee rag." Rinse the bandana in water 200 feet from a stream, and hang it on your pack to dry.

A "backcountry bidet" is a popular option. A small squeeze bottle with water and concentrated soap such as Dr. Bronner's works well. Use the right hand to squeeze the container and the left hand to clean the appropriate areas.

With all these techniques, clean your hands with hand sanitizer after using the bathroom.

PRIVACY IN THE DESERT

Those who value privacy may feel panicky about the notion of going to the bathroom on a backpacking trip in the desert, where wide-open spaces and minimal vegetation don't offer much cover.

But scrub brush and other hearty plants create potential visual barriers, and most desert landscapes aren't completely flat; dips and hills provide a little privacy. Take advantage of this natural cover. Ask your trip partners to keep an eye out for any oncoming people.

Remember that desert ecosystems are very fragile. Most land agencies now require people to pack out their used toilet paper. Use the steps provided earlier in this chapter on hygiene (page 101); what may seem a bit "yucky" is just another step to perform on the learning curve of backpacking. If you can file your taxes, you can definitely learn how to pack out toilet paper. Ergo, you'll survive.

Bedtime Checklist

Before going to bed, make sure to finish all the camp chores. Cross all your Ts by checking this list:

❑ **Use the bathroom, clean yourself up, and brush your teeth.** Don't skimp on basic hygiene.

❑ **Securely store trash, leftover food, and food-scented toiletries like toothpaste.** Put such items in a food locker or bear bag, or tie a food bag to a tree where there is no megafauna. Consult the backcountry office on the proper food storage techniques for the area.

❑ **If you had a campfire, make sure the fire is completely out.**

❑ **Collect all your gear inside the tent, or secure it elsewhere.** You do not need your equipment blowing away at night.

❑ **Filter or treat any water.** You may want a drink at night, and you'll want to have it ready for breakfast.

❑ **Look over the map to see your route for the following day.** Make a note of challenging climbs or scenic highlights you want to explore.

❑ **Check in with trip partners.** See if anyone has issues or concerns for the morning hike.

❑ **Stretch before going to bed.** Stretching keeps the muscles loose and limber. You are less likely to have an injury. A simple and effective stretch is to grab the back of your ankle and lift it toward your back while standing on one foot.

❏ **In your tent, remove the insoles from your shoes.** This allows your shoes to dry out more.

❏ **If it's cold, change into thermal tops and bottoms and dry socks.** Wearing a wool hat or fleece beanie to bed will always keep you warm, too.

❏ **Stage your hiking clothes for the next day.** Avoid wasting time in the morning looking for where you placed the clothes the night before. Place your shoes just outside the tent underneath the rainfly or vestibule.

❏ **Read, relax, and sleep.** You'll be refreshed for the following day's journey.

❏ **Place your headlamp and water bottle by your head.** Many tents have an inside pocket that makes an ideal location for these items.

Getting Proper Sleep

If you're not able to sleep at night, you will be exhausted during your hike the next day. In theory, you would think hiking all day would make it easier to sleep. But sometimes it's difficult to sleep in unfamiliar places where there are new noises.

Here are some tips for getting a good night's sleep:

Fuel your body with enough food, and stay hydrated. A full stomach means you have enough fuel to recover at night, and a hydrated body means you can process this fuel efficiently. If you are hungry and dehydrated, you will find that it is difficult to sleep.

Don't drink alcohol. Alcohol will dehydrate you and prevent a good night's sleep.

Avoid caffeinated beverages at night. Caffeine will keep you awake.

Stick to your routine. Go to bed and get up at your standard time. Your body clock will be out of sync if you try to force yourself to go to bed earlier. If you are a night owl, consider adjusting your home hours while you are physically preparing for the trail.

Buy a thicker sleeping pad. A thicker and more comfortable sleep pad may help you sleep. A thin foam mattress might be lighter, but if you can't sleep, the saved ounces will not matter.

Bring some earplugs. Blocking out the sounds you are not used to (or a snoring tentmate) might be what you need to catch some much-needed Zs.

Breaking Down Camp

After breakfast with a cup of joe, it's time to break camp and pack up for the morning hike.

Breaking camp is the inverse of making camp in many ways—you pack up your gear and then check the campsite to make sure no equipment is left behind.

First, pack up your tent, sleeping pad, and sleeping bag. Check the shelter to make sure there are no loose items left inside. Shake out any debris before packing the tent; a dirty tent will not last as long and can even be damaged if dirt is left inside. Roll up the tent and place it back in its bag.

Then, pack up your gear. Remember to load your pack as directed earlier in the book (page 57). Many who tend to pack up quickly to get back on the trail don't pack as efficiently and regret it later. Take your time and pack correctly; you'll save time and not have to stop to readjust your pack. When packing up gear and cooking breakfast, be mindful of nearby campers. You might be tempted to shout a "barbaric yawp" over the tent tops, but your neighbors likely won't appreciate it.

Next, perform a sweep of the campsite. Make sure all stray wrappers or other garbage is picked up. Remember, even food scraps must be packed out. Look for gear you may have forgotten, such as hiking poles. If you had a fire, be absolutely sure that it's out. It only takes one hot coal to start a wildfire, and you'll be slapped with some hefty fines.

With chores completed, it's time to hit the trail.

Wrapping Up Your Trip

Congratulations! You've finished your first trip in the wild, and not only did you survive—you thrived! You're going home with memories that will last for years—that campsite near a pristine trout-filled stream, or that climb to the top of a pass where you saw nothing but an endless vista of mountains.

After you arrive back at the trailhead, the adventure isn't over; it's time to fill your belly, quench your thirst, and celebrate the fantastic journey that you just enjoyed. You might find that your first post-trip burger and beer are the best you've ever tasted.

Don't forget an essential part of your post-trip ritual: Once you have cell-phone reception, let your friends or family know you are back safely. After you get home and take a gloriously refreshing shower, look over the photos and share them with friends. You'll likely be thinking about your next trip already, pondering new mountains to climb or lakes to discover. Onward, and happy trails!

BASIC FIRST AID

First-aid training is a broad topic that could fill a book or class on its own. First aid can range from draining a blister to treating heat exhaustion to performing CPR on a heart-attack victim. A page or two of summaries won't do the topic justice.

Instead, plan to take a first-aid course offered by a local Red Cross chapter. Better yet, consider taking a wilderness first-aid class provided by organizations like Wilderness Medicine Institute. Weekend classes are 16 hours long and will provide you with the skills you'll need to assess a situation and possibly stabilize a patient until more qualified assistance arrives. Search "wilderness first-aid class near me" online to find one.

If you can't attend a course, then buy a wilderness first-aid book by one of the organizations that teach the class. This book is no substitute for classroom learning, but you'll at least have some knowledge.

In wilderness first-aid situations, follow these key steps:

Survey the scene. Is the scene safe for you, the rescuers, and the victims? You do not want to injure yourself and other rescuers or add to the victim's injuries. Also, note the type of injury or damage in case you need to brief other rescuers. Most important, note what resources are available if the patient needs to be evacuated. Are there enough people to help carry out the person? Perhaps there's a high point one mile up the trail where there is cell-phone reception? Many cell phones have an emergency mode that will work even if your own carrier isn't receiving service, but don't count on that. Note that dedicated emergency communication devices will work where there is no cell-phone reception and are an increasingly popular option in remote areas. Research online for more information about these tools.

Realistically evaluate your abilities. You can easily treat a shallow cut in the field. But managing a significant chest wound is likely beyond your abilities unless you have the proper training and the right equipment.

Know when to evacuate a patient. A correctly treated blister does not mean your trip is over. A sprained ankle might mean you have to walk out with the help of friends. But if a person suffers a stroke, you'll need to get help ASAP. Know the signs of such injuries, and do your best to triage accurately. In these situations, minutes and even seconds count. Always, always have a plan of action in place for the unthinkable.

Wilderness medicine focuses on stabilizing the victim rather than treatment. Remember, people with more training and equipment will take over treating severe injuries at some point. A small first-aid kit consisting of adhesive bandages in assorted sizes, gauze pads, medical tape, pain medication, safety pins, and tweezers is a must on any backpacking trip. Purchasing a commercial kit is an option, but a homemade first-aid kit can be made using many items around the house. Homemade kits are usually lighter and cheaper, too. Repurpose items like hiking poles and bandanas to make splints. These treatments will help stabilize a patient with more extensive injuries until emergency help arrives.

TRIPS FOR FIRST-TIME BACKPACKERS

Alabama: DeSoto State Park's network of trails link together to form trips appropriate for weekends.

Alaska: If you have time available, the South Fork Valley Trail near Anchorage delivers world-class scenery, and the logistics are relatively easy.

Arizona: The Superstition Mountains outside of Phoenix are easy to get to and provide some stunning desert scenery. Hiking the Lost Dutchman's Gold Mine trail is always memorable.

Arkansas: The Centerpoint Trail in the Ozarks offers some of the steepest bluffs west of the Mississippi.

California: Henry W. Coe State Park is in the middle of the state and features spring wildflowers, easy trails, and great views from the ridges.

Colorado: There are so many choices in the Rocky Mountain state. The Bison and McCurdy Ridge in Lost Creek Wilderness offers unique and worthwhile views. The ridge traverses a plateau full of red rock with great views when other mountains are snow covered.

Connecticut: The Appalachian Trail in Connecticut feels scenic and remote. Consider doing an out-and-back of a set distance on arguably the most famous of all footpaths.

Delaware: White Clay Creek State Park offers 20 miles of trails in a historical setting.

Florida: Big Cypress National Preserve offers what is arguably the most scenic hiking through pristine wetlands.

Georgia: Amicalola Falls State Park is home to the approach trail of the famous Appalachian Trail; it also features scenic waterfalls, rolling green hills, and ridge views. Trails link together to form a 20-mile loop.

Hawaii: Logistics make this state a hard one for beginners, but the Kalalau Trail is a bucket list item for beginners and experienced backpackers alike.

Idaho: The Pettit and Toxaway Lakes Loop near Ketchum features 18 miles of stunning scenery.

Illinois: Starved Rock State Park offers some of the most scenic hiking in Illinois.

Indiana: A section of the well-known Knobstone Trail makes a great trip in fall.

Iowa: Check out Yellow River State Forest for some backpacking ideas.

Kansas: The Elk River Trail draws most Kansas backpackers looking for a bit of wildness in their state.

Kentucky: Red River Gorge is known for climbing, but it also has scenic trails that beckon hikers.

Louisiana: The 24-mile Wild Azalea Trail is a national recreation trail in a state noted more for paddle sports than backpacking. But when the path's namesake flower is in full bloom, this hike is a wildflower lover's delight.

Maine: Baxter State Park is only five hours from Boston, yet it is as wild and remote as the American West. The network of trails is suitable for hikers of all levels.

Maryland: Catoctin Mountain Park offers a delightful wooded hiking experience.

Massachusetts: In the Berkshires, Mount Greylock State Reservation's Hopper Trail has a loop that takes in the impressive Money Brook Falls and some of the last East Coast old growth forest. Mount Greylock is also the highest point in the state.

Michigan: The Manistee River Trail and North Country Trail Loop in Michigan's Lower Peninsula consistently rank as "best of" trails in the area.

Minnesota: Sections of the Superior Hiking Trail offer the most accessible hikes for a beginner.

Mississippi: For some of the best backpacking in Mississippi, check out the Black Creek National Recreation Trail.

Missouri: The 17-mile Mudlick Trail goes through some of the geologically oldest landscape in the United States.

Montana: Glacier National Park is arguably Montana's main attraction, but it is more remote, and grizzly bear activity might scare off beginners. Instead, consider Yellowstone National Park with its more benign terrain. Grizzly bear areas can't be avoided in the Montana mountains; contact Yellowstone to get thorough information about hiking in grizzly territory.

Nebraska: The Soldier Creek Wilderness Area in the Pine Ridge Escarpment belies Nebraska's reputation as a land of cornfields and flat plains. The Soldier Creek Wilderness has streams and buttes, and you might even see reintroduced bighorn sheep.

Nevada: The Nevada side of Lake Tahoe offers logistically easy hiking not far from Reno.

New Hampshire: Some of the most stunning terrain in New England exists in the White Mountains. The Appalachian Mountain Club shuttle makes one-way hikes of various lengths easy to access. The Franconia Ridge Loop is arguably the highlight of this area.

New Jersey: The scenic Delaware Water Gap National Recreation Area will not disappoint anyone who enjoys backpacking.

New Mexico: The Pecos Wilderness, with its 13,000-plus-foot peaks, alpine lakes, and bighorn sheep, never ceases to amaze hikers.

New York: Instead of the famous Adirondack High Peaks region, go to the Catskills for easier hiking on less crowded trails.

North Carolina: Backpacking in the Nantahala National Forest offers scenic balds (mountains with no tree cover) and ample spring wildflowers.

North Dakota: Theodore Roosevelt National Park on the High Plains is a fitting tribute to the rough-riding president and a great place for beginning hikers to explore.

Ohio: The Shawnee State Forest contains Ohio's most famous and scenic hiking trails.

Oklahoma: Check out the Ouachita Mountains near Tulsa when the mountains in the rest of the country are still snow-covered.

Oregon: The Lakes Basin is called the "Swiss Alps of Oregon," and it's easy to see why. These trails are accessible and loaded with dynamic scenery, making this area perfect for backpackers of all levels.

Pennsylvania: Old Logger's Path in eastern Pennsylvania is a loop trail through moderate terrain.

Rhode Island: Arcadia Management Area pops with fall colors in October. Of particular note is the area around Breakheart Pond.

South Carolina: Table Rock State Park features a 17-mile hike to the highest peak in South Carolina, Sassafras Mountain.

South Dakota: In the Black Hills, climb to the top of Black Elk Peak to summit the highest peak east of the Mississippi.

Tennessee: South Cumberland State Park offers a variety of trails that are less crowded than the Smokies or nearby areas on the Appalachian Trail.

Texas: Caprock Canyons State Park in the Texas Panhandle is worth savoring. The park has a long canyon deep in the High Plains with backcountry campsites and a herd of free-range bison.

Utah: Utah's canyon country is unlike any other terrain in North America. And a backpacking trip in Chesler Park at Canyonlands Needles District is a great way to experience it.

Vermont: Camel's Hump State Park lends itself to autumn color. The trails traverse the second highest, undeveloped mountain in Vermont.

Virginia: Grayson Highlands State Park reminds many people of an American West landscape with its open vistas and grazing ponies.

Washington: Olympic National Park, a unique landscape where the mountains meet the sea, is worth seeing.

West Virginia: The Dolly Sods Wilderness is another southern Appalachian area that looks like a Western landscape with its craggy-looking peaks and open vistas.

Wisconsin: The Kettle Moraine State Forest contains 60 miles of hiking and some of Wisconsin's most remote-feeling terrain.

Wyoming: Holly Lake in Grand Teton National Park is scenic, and is not far from Jackson, Wyoming. This makes for easier logistics, and requires much less planning than other places in this remote state.

SPRING

NORTHWEST
Lower elevation canyons provide solitude and spring flowers.

CENTRAL WEST COAST
View wildlife in the Coastal Redwoods.

SOUTHWEST
Temperatures are moderate, and the streams and freshwater springs flow reliably. Night skies are perfect for stargazing.

ROCKIES
Stay in lower elevations to avoid lasting snow. The fishing is excellent.

MIDWEST
The bird migration is nirvana for birdwatchers.

NORTHEAST
"Mud season" can make for a messy, uncomfortable trip.

SOUTHEAST
Savor the first wildflowers of the season.

SUMMER

NORTHWEST
Snowcapped peaks are framed by summer wildflowers.

CENTRAL WEST COAST
The High Sierras offer gorgeous alpine-style lakes; bring a fishing rod.

SOUTHWEST
Summer backpacking is not recommended for beginners because of hot, unpredictable weather and intense sun exposure.

ROCKIES
Enjoy wildflowers and waterfalls galore.

MIDWEST
Lakes are the perfect temperature for afternoon swims.

NORTHEAST
The days are long, and the fish are biting.

SOUTHEAST
Creekside hiking and lush foliage offer respite from the heat.

FALL

NORTHWEST
Hear the sound of mating elks, called *bugling*, and see fall foliage.

CENTRAL WEST COAST
Moderate days and cool nighttime temperatures make for excellent backpacking conditions.

SOUTHWEST
Explore the area's famed slot canyons with little flash-flood danger.

ROCKIES
Aspen leaf-peeping makes for stunning photography.

MIDWEST
Add some canoeing to your trips and enjoy the many lakes.

NORTHEAST
Is anything more beautiful than New England in the fall?

SOUTHEAST
The summer heat is gone, replaced by fall's cool nights.

WINTER

NORTHWEST
Winter backpacking is not recommended for beginners.

CENTRAL WEST COAST
It's a perfect time of the year for trails near the ocean.

SOUTHWEST
In lower desert areas, such as Big Bend, expect perfect lighting for stunning photos.

ROCKIES
Winter backpacking is not recommended for beginners.

MIDWEST
There are fewer people out this time of year, which means easier access to otherwise busy areas.

NORTHEAST
Winter backpacking is not recommended for beginners.

SOUTHEAST
Solitude reigns, and less vegetation means the views are superb.

FIRST TRIP CHECKLIST

Here is a suggested gear list that works for three-season conditions. Use this list when purchasing gear or packing.

Clothing—Worn

❑ Boots or hiking shoes

❑ Synthetic T-shirt or long-sleeved shirt

❑ Synthetic shorts or long pants

❑ Wool or synthetic socks

❑ Sunglasses

❑ Sun hat, bandana

Bring sunscreen if you opt to forgo a hat, a long-sleeved shirt, or pants.

Clothing—Packed

❑ Rain jacket

❑ Rain mitts or gloves; dishwashing gloves are a budget alternative

❑ Rain pants

❑ Synthetic or wool long underwear top and bottom

❑ Fleece pullover or wind shirt

❑ Lightweight puffy jacket

❑ Wool or fleece hat

- ❏ Wool or fleece gloves or mittens

- ❏ One pair of hiking socks

- ❏ One pair of sleep socks

Primary Gear (for Each Person)

- ❏ Pack with pack liner

- ❏ Sleeping bag in stuff sack

- ❏ Sleeping pad

Primary Gear (Shareable)

- ❏ Shelter (a tent works best for first-time backpackers; two people can share a tent)

- ❏ Don't forget the tent poles and stakes.

- ❏ Stove

- ❏ Cooking pot (one liter for one person; two liters for two people)

- ❏ Water treatment gear (chemicals can be shared; more comfortable to share a filter)

Remaining Gear

- ❏ Bowl (if not eating out of cooking pot)

- ❏ Spoon

- ❏ Mug (optional, for hot drinks)

- ❏ Small tube of sunscreen (if not using clothing for primary sun protection)

- ❏ Hand sanitizer

- ❏ Toilet paper and potty trowel (bring resealable food bags and a plastic shopping bag if you are required to pack out TP)

- ❏ Pocket knife

- ❏ Lighter

- ❏ Compass

- ❏ Headlamp

- ❏ 2-liter CamelBak, or (2) 1-liter plastic bottles (take more containers if you need additional water for dousing a campfire or for drinking between water sources)

- ❏ Map

- ❏ Compass

- ❏ Small first-aid kit

- ❏ Bug spray (a head net is also helpful in particularly insect-prone areas like northern New England or the Sierras)

- ❏ Mobile device (optional)

- ❏ Battery pack (if you use more power from a mobile device for activities such as filming videos or listening to music)

- ❏ Food storage such as a bear canister or 50-foot cord to hang a food bag if required

Food for Three Days

- ❏ Three days of snacks

- ❏ Two breakfasts

- ❏ Two dinners

LIGHTWEIGHT BACKPACKING

Lightweight backpacking is not discussed in great detail in this book. There's no denying that the less weight you carry, the easier hiking becomes. However, if you take too little gear, your experience could become not only uncomfortable but dangerous.

Finding a balance between weight and comfort, minimalism and safety comes with experience. But there are some inexpensive, safe, and easy ways to lighten your load. If you shed a few ounces, the pounds will follow. The key to light backpacking is not the gear you take, but rather what you don't take. If you are out for three days, you don't need three pairs of underwear—bring one pair and rinse as needed. And don't buy the most massive backpack in the store. Few beginners go out for more than a few days at a time, so expedition packs are unnecessary. A smaller pack is less expensive and weighs less.

Finally, follow the checklist starting on page 125. If you keep your items to a minimum, your overall pack weight will be low without having to buy specialized lightweight gear.

RESOURCES

The following books, websites, and resources are informative, insightful, and entertaining. They will enhance your overall appreciation of the outdoors, so check them out.

Navigation: The Columbia River Orienteering Club (CROC) is a Washington-based outdoor group that has an excellent 18-part YouTube tutorial on navigation. The videos cover map and compass use, declination, using a GPS, and other topics that all backcountry users should know about when venturing into our wild lands. Visit bit.ly/2GRYPxV to see this playlist.

CalTopo.com is a free, powerful website for plotting out and creating routes. With maps available online, you can create and print the appropriate resources for your adventures. Paired with CalTopo, the Gaia GPS app complements the traditional paper map used for navigation.

Places to go: The Hiking Project (hikingproject.com) is a free online trip database that has both short hikes for training and longer routes for backpacking. In addition to route descriptions and specifications, you can download and print maps and GPS waypoints. Summit Post (summitpost.com) is another website that gives excellent information for specific areas. For example, if you wanted to hike the Mummy Range in Rocky Mountain National Park, the site would provide you with popular trail and route information, as well as requirements for permits, bear canisters, and other pertinent info for trip planning.

Lightweight backpacking: Mike Clelland's *Ultralight Backpackin' Tips* is an inexpensive, quick read that provides practical ideas for trimming backpack weight without spending a lot of money or time.

Budget Outdoor Gear: For extensive reviews on budget gear, visit my website at pmags.com/tag/cheap-outdoor-gear. I discuss options available at surplus stores, discount warehouses such as Costco, and even hardware stores. There are many options for inexpensive, light, and effective gear and clothing, so you don't have to break the bank.

Advanced Backpacking Techniques: Cam Honan (thehikinglife.com), Andrew Skurka (andrewskurka.com), and Liz Thomas (eathomas.com) have websites and other resources, including online classes and articles available to explore tips and techniques, or to help plan long walks. All three hikers are accomplished outdoors people who not only achieve incredible athletic feats, but inspire and provide extensive information to help you plan your adventures.

Women's Backpacking Questions: The closed Facebook group, "All Women All Trails: Hiking & Backpacking" states: "Novice to expert, this group is for women worldwide who want to spend time on trails hiking, backpacking, or trail running! We're about sharing info and encouraging each other." https://www.facebook.com/groups/allwomenalltrails/

Hiking with Dogs: The "Hiking with Dogs" public Facebook group is the place to find answers about logistics, health, gear,

or other issues related to taking your pup into the backcountry.
https://www.facebook.com/groups/9003421258/

Inspiration: The "who, what, where, and how" are important parts of the backpacking experience. But the "why" is often the reason we go backpacking. Some books to inspire you along these lines include *Desert Solitaire* by Edward Abbey, *The Man Who Walked Through Time* by Colin Fletcher, and *Red* by Terry Tempest Williams.

INDEX

ACKNOWLEDGMENTS

Thanks to my editor, Justin Hartung, for his patience and guidance during this process. A big thank you to the hiking community for sharing their knowledge, ideas, and insights over the years. I'd like to thank my family for accepting that writing, guiding, and hiking a lot makes more sense for their son, brother, nephew, and cousin than continuing to work in a beige box. A huge thank you to my friends who not only hiked with me over the years, but shared a pint and some laughs, and have always been there for me through bad times and the increasingly good times. And special thanks to Joan; her encouragement and love helped more than Snickers bars. And that's saying a lot.

ABOUT THE AUTHOR

 **Paul Magnanti** is an avid outdoors person based in Moab, Utah. He's completed "The Triple Crown of Backpacking" —the Appalachian, Pacific Crest, and Continental Divide Trails—and regional trails such as the Great Divide Trail in the Canadian Rockies, the Colorado Trail, a solo backpacking trip across Utah, and many other longer walks.

Paul enjoys backcountry skiing, dispersed camping in remote areas, backpacking whenever he can, and exploring Ancient Puebloan sites. When not out in the backcountry, Paul is searching for the perfect pint, eating the most scrumptious post-trail burger, or trying to find the best chile relleno. Paul can be found online at PMags.com.